T0077473

NO MORE
MS DEPRESSION
MS-102

Finding the Pieces to Your Puzzle

RAMON HYRON GARCIA

BALBOA.
PRESS

A DIVISION OF HAY HOUSE

Copyright © 2014 Ramon Hyron Garcia.

All rights reserved. No part of this book may be used or reproduced by any means, graphic, electronic, or mechanical, including photocopying, recording, taping or by any information storage retrieval system without the written permission of the publisher except in the case of brief quotations embodied in critical articles and reviews.

Balboa Press books may be ordered through booksellers or by contacting:

Balboa Press
A Division of Hay House
1663 Liberty Drive
Bloomington, IN 47403
www.balboapress.com
1 (877) 407-4847

Because of the dynamic nature of the Internet, any web addresses or links contained in this book may have changed since publication and may no longer be valid. The views expressed in this work are solely those of the author and do not necessarily reflect the views of the publisher, and the publisher hereby disclaims any responsibility for them.

The author of this book does not dispense medical advice or prescribe the use of any technique as a form of treatment for physical, emotional, or medical problems without the advice of a physician, either directly or indirectly. The intent of the author is only to offer information of a general nature to help you in your quest for emotional and spiritual well-being. In the event you use any of the information in this book for yourself, which is your constitutional right, the author and the publisher assume no responsibility for your actions.

Any people depicted in stock imagery provided by Thinkstock are models, and such images are being used for illustrative purposes only. Certain stock imagery © Thinkstock.

Printed in the United States of America.

ISBN: 978-1-4525-2362-0 (sc)
ISBN: 978-1-4525-2361-3 (e)

Balboa Press rev. date: 11/21/2014

CONTENTS

FOREWORD

By Rae Edwards
Founder & President/CEO of
MSstation™ Inc.
& Multiple Sclerosis Radio™

From the time I met Ray Garcia I knew he was a phenomenal man. Ray is a brilliant Author and a highly recognized inspirational speaker. We had the great honor and privilege of featuring Ray Garcia as MSstation™ Book Club's Author of the Month. After Ray explained "**No More MS Depression MS 101**" will be a three part series I became ecstatic! I recently finished reading "**No**

More MS Depression MS 101" 1 and 2 and I absolutely loved them! I am extremely eager to read part 3 now!

Ray Garcia is "dealing" (as he so keenly refers to this unpredictable journey) with Multiple Sclerosis admirably. Ray's strengths and accomplishments are unsurpassed. I marvel at his knowledge of treating MS alternatively. Ray basically returned from living in a hospice, where everyone may have simply given up on him, to becoming a motivational teacher and a successful Author.

Ray thank you for all you do for the Multiple Sclerosis Community. We need more individuals like you to not only share your knowledge but to also lead by example. Your Philosophy and Theories for fighting Multiple Sclerosis are remarkable and worth everyone with and without a Chronic Illnesses to explore.

Rae Edwards Founder and President of Multiple Sclerosis Radio™ MSstation™ Inc. www.MultipleSclerosisRadio.com

RECOMMENDATION

By Judi Lecoq

Vice President & Director of

Multiple Sclerosis Radio™

When Ramon asked me to write the forward for this book, I was and am truly honored. I, like Ramon, am living with this pesky companion called Multiple Sclerosis and I deeply connect with his uplifting, proactive message.

In my role as the Director of Multiple Sclerosis Radio, I interviewed Ramon and Jackie Joy, who contributed to this book as well as the first book, **No More MS Depression, MS-101**. I quickly realized that Ramon has an inspirational story, and so much to teach us in this struggle with MS. In his **No More MS Depression, MS-101**, Ramon takes us from living in hospice in 2010 to walking more than 5 miles a day. How did he do this? I mean, seriously!!!

In book 1, we learn about the different elements in the total approach that changed Ramon's life, beginning with a positive mental attitude. In the next book, this book**, No More MS Depression, MS-102**, Ramon takes us more in depth as he offers us more tools to help fight Multiple Sclerosis. I have to say that his books contain advice and information that can help people dealing with many health issues, but especially Multiple Sclerosis.

For me, this book speaks to me in my MS journey, and I feel inspired to keep up the fight.

Thank you Ramon.

Judi Lecoq
Vice President & Director of Multiple Sclerosis Radio™
www.MultipleSclerosisRadio.com

WHY I WROTE THIS 2ND BOOK

This book was inspired by a number of people, looking around I see too many people giving up, this just is not acceptable me. So when I had to deal with my own demons, I.E when I fell sick with my last relapse I wanted to give up. I found new ways by researching therapy, to heal myself and I read the Bible, knowing not to give up and not to speak negativity into existence. So I wrote this 2nd book as a compliment to the 1st book <beginner's guide> to show that there is hope. Just have faith in God and yourself, know that you are stronger than what you believe and there will be others out there who want you to be weaker than you believe. This book is to show how I became stronger than what others said and do what others said I would not be able to do. Now I hope you learn a lot from this book and start doing your own research. This is just an outline that you will use towards your goals and fill in the blanks to beat your own battles. Never give up and never let someone tell you what you can or cannot do. Do it, you got it.

This is why I wrote this book to help us have hope and to give strength to the weak. You can and you will, look every day in the mirror and say "I can, I will and I'm strong". Never give up, know that you are what you say you are and do not accept the things in life you do not want to accept. Accepting is a sign that you give up.

INTRODUCTION

First I'm no medical professional, these are my stories, my theories and my opinions. Please seek additional medical help if needed. This is just my story and how I dealt with MS in my life. I just want to share my story and give hope to the hopeless.

HI, my name is Ramon Hyron Garcia, I'm a 37 year old divorced father of 1 boy. I was adopted at 2 days old by an African American family!

I also DEAL WITH RRMS <relapsing remitting Multiple Sclerosis> and was diagnosed in 2003 at

Loma Linda Medical Center in beautiful southern California.

This is my story part#2 of how I took grim news 7 years after my diagnosis and made it work out in my favor! I hope and pray you all can take wisdom from my weakness and strength to forge your own armor to fight through the depression and negative thoughts that this HORRIBLE disease brings!

I also want to share how I went from 275+ lbs. to 202 lbs. in 7 months or less, bounced back up to 280 and now I am back down to 250 and from NOT being able to do 10 pushups to being able to do 120+ a day. Feeling the loneliness that NO ONE understands on to helping others cope with the same issues, now my mail box and phone does NOT stop with 'positive messages'....

Sunday morning like the 4 others before it, I walked out my front door to go to church. ALL of a sudden I fell backwards and could NOT move. I had to lay there for 3 hours before my next door neighbor finally helped me back into the house, at which time he took me to the ER and they just wrote it of as Bell's Palsy. OK, I had denied MS since 2003, it is now December 2009. SO, having not taken care of myself, smoking, a horrible diet and STRESS did a number on me.

NOW I was sent home from the ER with medicine to treat Bell's Palsy, NOT MS. I was steadily getting worse. I became so weak I could not sit up without help and I lost all vision in my left eye. After 2 months of ER trips, I just gave up!

ONE day around March 1st I wanted to get out of my bed, <granted, remember I need help to even move> I tried to go to the rest room, I fell out of my bed and my cell phone was on my bed still.

I tried for the next 4 to 5 hours to do everything I could to get it. As a lot of you know when you use energy In MS you DO NOT GET IT BACK right away. Once I finally fetched my phone I dialed 911.

THEN it took me 2 hours to arm-crawl to the door to let in the EMT's all the while BEGGING the 911 dispatch operator NOT to let them break my door in!

NOW in the ER, they of course ran every test in the book. I swear I was a pin cushion.

The doctor ordered an MRI for the next morning. I still denied I had MS or was diagnosed with it so they had NO clue to look for it.

After a night of incontinence and blood draws, being asked to wake up every 2 hours for blood pressure and NEW pills to take, by the time 8 am rolled around I was off to take a MRI. After 1 ½ hours of being in that coffin, they confirmed MS almost immediately.

So now I'm in my hospital bed, unable to move, blind in 1 eye and I cannot use my voice now. The Neurologist doctor ordered me to go to rehab to see if I could regain my old self.

I'll tell you right now being trapped in your own thoughts is the scariest movie you could ever imagine.

OK now I am transferred to the rehab floor, I had probably 6 doctors come in and tell me I have to see this other doctor and do these other tests...... I did not know any better, NOR did I have any family there to help.

SO starts my new life after 30 years of being "normal". Having to relearn to walk, minor motor skills, even things like dressing myself to brushing my teeth, to even relearning how to use the restroom…. Had to visit a mock apartment to see if it was safe for me to transfer to the toilet, to the tub, to the sink WHILE in a wheel chair…

In psychiatric care, I kept a journal on EVERYTHING. My goals and how to become what I was. I honestly believe there was almost MORE stress there trying to get help.

Well 2 months passed and I can now WALK with a walker for a short period of time, but mostly my life at the time is in a wheel chair. For some reason unknown to me I was told I was being transferred to a hospice…

The hospice. I had no idea what this was ……. They told me it was a "nursing care facility to continue my rehab", ya right! I was the youngest person ever to go there, even the nurses were over

42 years if age, the next youngest patient was 63 years of age and I was just 31......

At this point I told myself I was NOT going to stop until I walked on my own and got out on my own!

So now I left the hospice, YES YES I WALKED OUT on my OWN. Got on a Greyhound Bus headed to Las Vegas, where I spent the next year continuing to work out where ever I could and I also was blessed to have a pool to use at my leisure. After a year of working out where ever I could at home and in the pool, I finally spoke to my cousin about getting out 100% on my own, so we looked for apartments. After a month or 2 he talked me into finding a home or renting out a room, so I found one with a nice lady who will remain nameless. She was younger then I was and was a female body builder and a health NUT, so between her knowledge and what I had learned watching videos and reading everything written by Dr. Terry Wahls, we crafted a diet that worked best for me and we would talk every day. It started to make sense that MS was a puzzle although WE or I did not call it that. I did not really coin that phrase until after 1.5 yrs. I moved to Milwaukee, Wisconsin with Jackie Joy.

She offered me a room for rent at a lower price then I was paying and I started helping her regain her life as well as continuing to rebuild mine and that's where I wrote **No More MS depression MS 101** and now this is the 2nd part of a 3-part series. I pray and hope you find the PIECES to YOUR puzzle called MS or depression or any of the negative effects in your life!

CHAPTER 1

HOW TO USE THE INFORMATION IN THIS BOOK

This book to some may be A LOT of information, especially since this is part #2 of my 3 part series. #1 was **No More MS Depression MS-101**, these are the theories I came to know and use throughout my journey in dealing with MS from 2009/10 until now. Part #3 will be what I have learned and built upon as well as what I have learned in years past.

You will read such things like I NEVER claim MS by saying I HAVE MS, I say things like I DEAL with MS or as my great friend Judi says "it's my unwanted friend". ALSO, by NO means do I claim to be a MEDICAL professional BUT urge folks to find what I call the pieces to THEIR puzzle we know as MS.

SO understand YOU need to WANT to do this, I mean that Multiple Sclerosis is not an easy road to walk. SO UNDERSTAND I also CRIED and wanted to quit or give up. BUT no matter how tough it is, I FOUND I AM and YOU are TOUGHER... YOU can DO THIS!

I hope you take this book and underline, highlight and take notes to start to put the pieces to your puzzle together. Do YOUR OWN research, experiment, get on Facebook or places like Muliplesclerosisradio.com for GREAT information on Multiple Sclerosis. FIND YOUR pieces. This book should be and I hope a GUIDE for you to start.

Thank YOU,
Ramon Hyron Garcia

READING NOTES

_____

_____

_____

_____

_____

_____

_____

_____

_____

_____

_____

_____

_____

_____

_____

_____

_____

MEDICAL DISCLAIMER

(1) No advice

This Book contains general information about medical conditions and treatments. The information is not advice and should not be treated as such.

(2) Credit

This document was created using a Legal template.

(3) No warranties

The medical information in this book is provided without any representations or warranties, express or implied. We make no representations or warranties in relation to the medical information in this book.

Without prejudice to the generality of the foregoing paragraph, we do not warrant or represent that the medical information in this book:

(a) will be constantly available, or available at all; or

(b) is complete, true, accurate, up to date or non-misleading.

(4) Professional assistance

You must not rely on the information in this book as an alternative to medical advice from your doctor or other professional healthcare provider.

If you have any specific questions about any medical matter, you should consult your doctor or other professional healthcare provider.

If you think you may be suffering from any medical condition, you should seek immediate medical attention.

You should never delay seeking medical advice, disregard medical advice or discontinue medical treatment because of information in this book.

(5) Limiting our liability

Nothing in this medical disclaimer will:

(a) limit or exclude our liability for death or personal injury resulting from negligence;
(b) limit or exclude our liability for fraud or fraudulent misrepresentation;
(c) limit any of our liabilities in any way that is not permitted under applicable law; or
(d) exclude any of our liabilities that may not be excluded under applicable law

CHAPTER 2

THE MANY WAYS I USED TO GET FRUSTRATED

I have found many ways to keep myself from getting frustrated, mostly I laugh at myself and I find a joke in everything I do. Like when a trip, I look back and say "who put that there?" knowing I tripped over my own feet or air with the imaginary llama that somehow wandered into my home. I also remember to tell myself I deal with MS and that alone is enough to make a person frustrated.

But I know to smile because I may have tripped but I'm not dead, so I can get up and try again where this would have frustrated others, I find a way to just laugh. There are plenty of ways to make a horrible situation better in your mind, you just need to be like a child and use your imagination. Remember if you feel comfortable it makes everyone else feel comfortable, not saying that you need their approval. But it does help your self-esteem when you build yourself up, not in the self-absorbed conceded way for then no one can tear you down.

As my mom would say "sending your own wood up to heaven, building your bridge strong, do not let others tear down what you have built". Now these are a few ways I see things. I also look inward for my faith in God and Jesus Christ.

Now I know that might not be everyone's view, but this how I do it. So find your way, find your funny, do what works for you. What I'm basically trying to say is find YOUR piece<s> to the puzzle we call MS.

Another way I forget about MS for a short period of time is that I play games. More specifically online games, like World of Warcraft or Star Wars Old Republic. These things keep me calm and for the one, two or three hours I am immersed in the world of the character that does not deal with MS or diabetes or lupus and possesses super-powers.

We have many things in the world that continuously have a way of making us focus entirely on the negative, so I'm hoping to show how we need to focus on the positive which was part of the reason I wrote the book **No More MS Depression MS 101**. Not only to show folks that there are many natural ways to add to the regiment of fighting this horrible disease but there's a way for us to beat the depression that MS causes with everything we see in the world, only to get frustrated and then we tend always to focus on the negatives of life, hence the negatives in MS and all the negative things it brings to the table. But this table seats two, so I asked what are you bringing to the table that you find funny? Find what makes you laugh and bring that to the table and confuse MS and make it wonder what to do next.

So do not get frustrated and know that you control more than you thought, let's stop giving MS the power now. I know a lot of people are going to say "MS does have the power, it's in control", I say no YOU have the control, YOU are not dead, YOU make the choice. Think about it… MS does not make a decision, it does what it's supposed to do. Now, are you doing what you can to help your body fight back? Most people do not know half or even a quarter of what you can do for yourselves, but there have been many people before us that have written or discussed with others online or in a lecture or in a YouTube video, so there are many tools to get info on different pieces the puzzle. This puzzle in our life is called MS, find what pieces work for you.

So don't get frustrated, know that this is not a death sentence something they should of told you at diagnosis, but in my theory that doesn't make money, this in itself is frustrating. So this truth brings another piece of why I wrote this book and why I will be writing book number three. In book #1 I've tried to show how I began my fight and put my pieces of the MS puzzle together. I use things like adjusting my diet because of Dr. Wahls, but I had to adjust what worked for her to work for me and that is my hope and prayer that you would do so too. Please know and understand that I know and understand this may or may not work for you. The point of all this is to try everything. It saddens me to see so many who beg for help and then reject the help that is given. You cannot say it does not work if you have not tried it, like the great Michael Jordan said "you miss every shot you don't take". I feel the same words apply to diseases, how can you say this does not work if you never tried it? Now this might not work in reversing everything and just because you get CCSVI does not mean it is going to work, so be cautiously optimistic.

But let's get back to the topic, there are many ways to not get frustrated, so find something good. It might be watching funny videos on YouTube or it might be sitting on the porch reading a good book like this book =p. I surely hope you can find something that you are interested in that keeps your mind on what's good in life and not the fact that you are dealing with a horrible situation. This might also be watching your kids play in the yard or watching neighbor kids play in the street or maybe even do like I do in your mind and look at something and make it a short funny movie. I swear the cat that lives in this house calls me fat and tries to flip me off, but these are just ways I have found to make myself less frustrated. But I know many people will say this is a cop-out, but like I said find your way to get less frustrated and to find the funny in all that you do.

READING NOTES

CHAPTER 3

DO NOT BE DISCOURAGED

At times it feels like we are just hanging on by our finger tips. BUT you're still hanging on and that's what we need to focus on. YOU are not a quitter, otherwise you would have let go already. I know sometimes we want to. I have felt alone and abandoned. It is a feeling I don't wish on anyone, BUT we have made it through and WE are still here. For that reason we should look around and smile and remember it is ok to want to quit. But actually doing it is at that moment is a premature choice. BUT know we can choose next time to NOT give up and find a way to exercise a better grip that will be a little easier to hold onto.

In this I want to emphasize it is NOT OVER! You are still here to make things better. I know some of us feel as though we are walking in a maze with NO lights on anywhere and it seems for every step we take it's as though we have headed in the wrong direction. BUT I am here to help you understand that you are stronger and MORE than the diagnosis. You are made strong. It's difficult to self-motivate, I know. There were MANY nights I sat in the hospital unable to get up on my own and use the restroom or grab a drink from the kitchen. It was VERY frustrating to be a 31 year old man <at the time of the 2nd relapse> and to know I could not walk and talk as I once did. It tore into my self-esteem and it still does 4 years later. ALTHOUGH I'm 90% back to where I was, I will not be satisfied until I EXCEED where I was BEFORE all this happened to me. SO PLEASE set a goal for yourself and become a NEW creation. There are hardly any TIMES WE GET A 2ND CHANCE TO REMAKE OURSELVES, but the time is now. Delve into your minds and hearts and choose what you would love to make better and encourage yourself to do it. Also find a friend to help you see those WINS that you may not notice.

MS does what it can to discourage you. Like in the movie Harry Potter, Luna said "if I were him <in our case MS> I'd want you to feel alone, THEN you are not as much of a threat". Keep this in mind, it <MS> wants to divide your heart, soul and mind to make you think it is hopeless. BUT it is not, the fact you are reading this shows you will NOT lay down nor give up. But do not just close this book and think it over, YOUR fight MUST CONTINUE. This book is maybe a START or maybe an addition to help you piece together YOUR puzzle of MS.

READING NOTES

CHAPTER 4

LAUGHING AT YOURSELF AND MAKING NEGATIVITY MAD

ONE thing that MANY people dealing with MS overlook ALOT is the healing power of laughter. NOT only is it a way to STOP the stressing for a minute or two <STRESS is a HUGE problem for us> the ability to learn to smile and laugh where ever you can is a HARD road to travel. We are surrounded by things that tell us we are not good enough. Like take this to lose weight or take this to feel NORMAL..... WHAT?..... NORMAL?..... HONESTLY how is NORMAL defined? ALSO who is the person who decided what NORMAL was...? HELLO, EVERYONE is doing something to make them feel "NORMAL". SO be the first to laugh, be the first to point out what someone else does NOT understand to ease tension NOT only for them BUT for YOURSELF.

Just remember YOU'RE NOT DEAD, so why act like it... OK some have to be in a wheelchair when just 2 months ago they were running in a marathon... WELL instead of crying on how unfair it is <since crying will not change it> make a sign and put it on the back of your chair that reads 'RIDING DIRTY' or 'STOPS AT ALL RAILROAD CROSSINGS' or 'STOPS FOR COFFEE', then go out to that same marathon and give it your all WITH A HUGE SMILE on your face, turn on your cellphone with the external speakers on and have your own theme MUSIC. Then put a cape on the back of your chair to make it look like you are a SUPER hero. BE an INSPIRATION, NOT the look of desperation and I know that a child will see you and KNOW he also can do anything just by observing how STRONG and courageous YOU are when you have EVERYTHING working against you.

This will turn back on MS what MS was trying to do to you. SEE, MS confuses us into starting to question WHO we are. LET me tell you, YOU are the same PERSON but you might need a wheelchair, walker, cane or maybe you need MORE time or have to find the restrooms and exits. Make this YOUR game, like tell yourself and family or friends "TODAY I AM PEE MAN OR WOMAN, ABLE to get to a restroom in a single bound <and sometimes not>". BUT when you lighten up the tension not only does this make YOU worry less <STRESS> but it also makes others less tense about MS since 4 out of 10 do not understand MS and 10 out of 10 have NO clue the STRESS you DEAL WITH.

SO when you show yourself doing something that you should be giving up on <IN their mind> BUT have a better attitude with it and make it fun for yourself, it in turn makes it more acceptable to others. BUT know by doing this YOUR welfare comes FIRST, showing and helping others accept it is an extra benefit.

When you wake up and know today is a slow day, over play it, I mean like act like everything is slow like your batteries are dying. IF you wake up and your balance is way off <like mine is usually> act like you are that metal ball in a pin ball machine and everything you bump into make a <TING> noise and yell 300 points, DOUBLE POINTS. This will show MS that NO matter what it tries, EVEN if you're not ready for it YOU will be

GRATEFUL because YOU are ALIVE and YOU are a warrior. Also say to MS <Ooooooo, YOU thought I was just going to lay down and DIE, No No I'm "insert your name" LISTEN to my battle roar> then hit the snooze and go back to sleep :).

JUST know everything is a choice! EVEN not choosing is a choice... it is just one that we were too lazy to admit. SO you can choose to lay there and complain on how MS does this or that <WHICH IS OK> just complaining while refusing to help YOURSELF is not and frankly is probably what 85% of people do. LOOK around, if you cannot find someone or something to motivate you positively, look harder...... ALL I'm saying is FOR EVERY 5 reasons not to go there are 4 reasons TO GO and 90% of the time you have to look for them.

See quitting is easy, BUT to keep going takes a level of courage and ambition YOU have to find. JUST like finding reasons to laugh or smile… sometimes it doesn't take much to find some but sometimes it does. The point is ALWAYS look and you WILL find them. See EVEN in a STORM a rainbow is forming. MOST of the time we need to just wait it out and picture the rainbow in our own minds to keep us HAPPY until the rainbow reveals itself.

I make little movies in my head starring whatever <or whoever> I have at my disposal at the time. Let's just say my roommates CAT is nearby and I SWEAR he calls me the "FATMAN" but for some reason he has Eric Cartmens voice from that show Southpark, then while he's walking around I think of a FUNNY dialogue and play it in my head or narrate what the cat could possibly be thinking...... JUST little things like this for however long it will redirect your mind TO not think of whatever negativity that might be going on around you. SO you can start with something like that, THEN do it with YOURSELF and make LIGHT of a situation that can be made LIGHT of, BUT PLEASE do not make something that is serious in someone else's life LIGHT because remember JUST because you see it as NOTHING others may see it as LIFE ALTERING.

READING NOTES

CHAPTER 5

BATTLING YOUR MIND IN DEALING WITH MS

Our mind is a constant source of negative emotions, IF YOU LET IT, BUT If you go into this knowing it <the mind> is going to try to make you see ALL the negative things that could and WILL happen unless you DO NOT ALLOW it.

This is how I dealt with the fact that I had to wake up EVERY day for 2 months in a hospital and do Physical Therapy and Occupational Therapy, ALL the while my mind was trying to convince me it was impossible to walk again or even talk again or use the restroom on my own. But since I learned that my mind was going to fight me alongside multiple sclerosis and try to keep me sick and on a road that felt comfortable, I HYPED myself up and worked as HARD as I could to do the things my mind, multiple sclerosis and SOME doctors said I could not do.

They ALL said I would not get out of the wheel chair that I was destined to roll around in the rest of my life. WRONG! I would NEVER be able to live on my own. WRONG! There is no way I could get back to my old self, YOU know they were RIGHT! I will be BETTER than before. I will walk FURTHER, not only will I be able to live again but I'm going to write books and make my OWN living. I will start up a nonprofit and name it all NO MORE MS DEPRESSION!

See, your mind tells you that you cannot or you should not but 8 times out of 10 it does not match up with your heart and soul. There is an instinct that we have inside to NEVER give up but more often than not our minds make arguments that make sense BUT then it does not match up with the other pieces in our puzzle..... SO do we just quit? I did not. Now I'm the happiest I've been in a quite a while and it is just getting better. See I am still not stopping my mind by being defeated and depressed, I woke up my determination and will to find a way to be better than what OTHER people said I should or could be.

NEVER listen if your heart and soul DO NOT accept it because it is negative. See we need to understand our bodies have its OWN internal government. Your body, mind and heart <soul> are like the branches of government <Legislative, Judicial, Executive> in that it works best when all 3 are working together in agreement. Sometimes

1 of the 3 is against EVERYTHING the other 2 says and we need to find ways around it and push on for what is RIGHT in our lives. For me it was finding those pieces to the MS puzzle to shed light on the clouds that NEGATIVITY casts and to give me that umbrella to keep me dry in that storm. THE storm is not gone but I'm now able to walk without getting wet. Sometimes the rain hits me, BUT I can STILL walk FORWARD and not stop and give up. I will find my shelter and my dry place, I just need to keep going. If I were to quit I would just end up soaked and STILL be dealing with multiple sclerosis. Our mind is a constant source of negative emotion IF YOU LET IT, BUT if you go into this knowing it is going to try to make you see all the negative things that can and WILL happen if you ALLOW them. Knowing this gives us the upper hand we can now start prepping our minds towards goals and psyching ourselves up to be ready for the coming internal battle.

OK, it's like this. WE know how to put out fires but that does not mean it will not and cannot happen. Just like MS we start finding pieces to this puzzle to put out this flame like tingling or being able to walk better, BUT know it will find others areas to make fires. BUT guess what? We need to SEE the win of beating tingles or walking then we deal with the new fire KNOWING it can be beat by remembering what we have already done.

READING NOTES

CHAPTER 6

ONLY LISTEN TO YOUR HEART

Many people listen to their doctor or a friend or family member. WHICH I'm sure at times they get LUCKY and are spot on to what may be needed in YOUR life. WELL, I'm here to say PLEASE, PLEASE listen to your own HEART. THAT instinct will tell you what is best for YOU.

Everywhere we turn, we are made to believe someone who studied in an area is better qualified to tell YOU what YOU are feeling. NOW, YES we need them to HELP us when we have thought of all we could and need a new PERSPECTIVE, BUT do not allow someone to tell YOU that YOU feel a certain way. THIS simply will ALWAYS lead a professional in telling you to do some GENERAL management way of taking care of YOUR feelings, also more than likely leading to medication. BUT then I say listen to your heart! Ask yourself questions, ALWAYS question EVERYTHING, because the MORE you know the clearer things get.

8 out of 10 medical professionals prescribe meds within the first 10 minutes of your visit. Before they talk to you and before they GET to know the INTIMATE details of the issue YOU are dealing with. SINCE MS has MANY faces and manifests differently in EACH AND EVERY person, it's insane they still place EVERYONE that deals with MS in the same bucket. SO this is why you hear different things that have WORKED for

some and not others so much and in some cases did the exact opposite of what it was intended for OR they shipped you off to a HOSPICE <as in my case> because they just don't know. BUT I listened to my heart, I learned to question everything, WORKED hard where I could, continued to do work outs to help my ability to walk again, talk, eat and balance. NOW I'm on my own DOING things THEY <the medical team> said I would not be able to do like living on my own, walking 10+ miles, cooking and writing my 2nd book in a 3 part series ALL because I FOLLOWED my heart to understand that I am tougher then what THEY know. I know me. THEY only know what is seen, not felt in MY body. I knew deep down to not give up, roll over and let MS harm me more.

I did research to see if ANY one else figured a way out of the sand trap of MS. I found an unlimited number of stories on the web, ALSO videos on YouTube then started to take what I felt in my heart was helping THEM and applied it where needed in my case. THEN I knew that once we see MS as a GIANT puzzle and find pieces that work IN OUR OWN LIVES, we will see that no matter what puzzle piece YOU find maybe there is a picture of a VICTORY or a FINISH line. YES, MS is a HUGE PUZZLE that may not get fixed in your lifetime BUT there are pieces you KNOW you can find to help the race that you're in to be a little easier and feel a little less like you're running up a hill. There is no reason, I can see, for me to put myself through MORE unnecessary torture when there are things I can do to ease some symptoms in order to make it that much easier to get to the next piece and place it.

This puzzle that we are putting together, try to imagine it as the size of the USA and the pieces are 1/2 the size of the states and you have to PHYSICALLY put down the piece but you know once you have finished with that piece your mind and body are eased of the painful torture that MS causes. Look at ALL those, as I say BANDAIDS for MS. This and that pill or shot will do THIS OR THAT and it is not even a 100% chance that it will help because a certain percent of people are NOTHING like you. NOW this might be a HUGE piece to YOUR puzzle. This is why over and over I advise to ALWAYS do your own research to see if this sounds good for YOU and take a day or 2 to search YOUR own heart. Some of us use prayer <I DO> to make choices AFTER research is done. NEVER just take things at face value, MS has been around for 40+ years and even then they had articles proclaiming something close to a cure. Hmmm, in 40+ years they made GREAT advances but listen to your heart. WHY do they say YES TO ALL man made things BUT hardly TELL you about diet, Cannabis, CCSVI, STEM CELLS, exercise??

I am ALWAYS cautious about a so called 'professional' if they are close-minded to research. HOW is it that a MEDICAL professional who studied FACTS about the human body IGNORES facts about DIET?? Or EXERCISE?? It pains me to see HOPE right at our fingertips YET doctors are quick to STOMP that out and prescribe a medication. Then you will need 3 more medications just to counteract the 1st ones side effects, YET it has been shown they get a BONUS or kickback if they get some of us on some certain medications. I would NOT have an issue IF those same doctors where pushing a HEALTHY diet and exercise 1st. SEE, my heart tells me medication should be a LAST resort in NON life threatening cases! BUT the LOVE of money is the ROOT cause of EVIL. YES, to be a so-called MEDICAL PRO and care more about MONEY then HELP is EVIL! NOW NOT ALL are like this and if you SAY you're a doctor and DEAL with MS, then YOU should know ALL the possibilities not just one or two. For this would make you NOT a doctor but a student who still needs to learn.

BUT then we have GREAT DOCTORS like DOCTOR TERRY L. WAHLS who wrote the Forward in my first book **NO More MS Depression MS 101** and she has a HOST of GREAT books that show us through diet and exercise we ALSO can move from secondary progressive MS to PRETTY MUCH an indefinite remission. In many ways my story and hers are PROOF that HEALTHY lifestyle changes, exercise, determination and FAITH <mine is in GOD, if this is not you then FAITH in SELF!> can catapult you into LIVING again. She left her motorized tilt-wheel chair, I left my bed and hospice. She now can jog, I can walk an unlimited amount of miles IN THE HEAT, shop without the help of a person and be in a grocery store with no motor cart.

I tell you now without listening to my heart and knowing I am better than a diagnosis, I would probably still be in that hospice not getting better but still declining like the doctors predicted I would.

READING NOTES

CHAPTER 7

MAKE YOURSELF THINK!

We are under CONSTANT criticism either from ourselves or someone else. Dealing with MS or ANY other negative effect can make you eventually start to wonder or blame yourself for what's happening. It also can inadvertently make you lash out at those closest to you and I've known for YEARS that I blamed DEALING with MS as being a direct result to how I had not always been a good person.

SO I made excuses as to why bad stuff happens to me like when a flare up hit or ANY of the thousands of ways MS can beat you down, I just internalized it and made excuses and made reference to something I may have done to cause it. I blamed how I acted on the outside to the cause of what's happening inside. NOW I truly think if we expect good in our lives GOOD will come, but like ALL things we cannot not show up in the end and expect a gold medal without A LOT of hard practice and effort!

SEE, NOW I play this blame game in reverse. Instead of blaming and focusing on the negative, I look for ALL the GOOD that I have done or about to do and I see the fruits growing on my tree. SEE I am a FIRM believer in "YOU REAP WHAT YOU HAVE SOWN". SO we, for some reason have a NATURAL tendency to see only the negatives. But we should start practicing to see the POSITIVE things which not only will help to get rid of stress and you will notice YOU HAVE come a lot further than you thought because MS is doing WHATEVER it can to keep you focused on the BAD things to misguide you from seeing how those POSITIVE things are beating it up. SEE, I have learned 'Misery Loves Company' and most of us will agree this to be true, WELL MS wants us to be miserable thinking we cannot. When you get into a group and share the HAVE NOTs and CANNOTs, it is SAD to watch people who are WINNERS be cut down to complainers. NOW I know people will say stuff like "I'm just there for them" and "we all NEED to vent, get it off our chest", I understand that but if you do the same thing EVERY WEEK it's not a visitation it's now home.

I truly think instead of just trying to see how many people deal with this issue, LET'S rephrase it into things like, I NO LONGER DEAL WITH THIS AND THIS IS HOW I DID IT! ETC,

ETC, I am hoping to share what I have done so maybe it will help someone else to improve on and share it so that it helps another then they improve it... so forth and so on, until it's no longer an issue or becomes less of one. I'm in 100's of groups and I have been in some at my hospital and hospice with a licensed therapist and 95% of people do the same thing INSTEAD of trying to find info on how to help, they talk JUST about the negative. I would sit there and ask question after question to find out how everyone deals with the negatives and try to make their ideas work for me, now not all worked and a lot did but I tried it all hoping that it would. I kept what produced good results and threw out the rest. Now I am NOT in a hospice, I LIVE ON MY OWN and I walk wherever I want in ANY weather. The POINT is I see now what I CAN do not what I CAN'T do then I BLAME the GOOD on the fact MS might of at one time took my ability to walk, talk and even go to the bathroom on myself

BUT I was ALIVE and still able to use my brain. I played MS's game in reverse and used its own tricks to free me from the MS bondage.

YOU CAN TOO! Never give up! KNOW you are more than a diagnosis! BELIEVE in yourself!

I DO NOT OWN MS nor does it own me! I tell EVERYONE I DEAL with it because that's what I do, is wake up EVERYDAY and DEAL with the fact that I stumble and talk funny (it gets better or worse depending on temperature, stress and of course MY OWN OUTLOOK). It has been proven time and time again that if we look at things with a HAPPY heart or NON stressed mind it can affect how our own bodies react to the day or the situation. This is why I 100% believe to not claim NEGATIVITY!!

NOW I know some will say "YOU ARE IN DENIAL", NO I never ONCE said I do not

DEAL with MS at all, I just choose to see it as something I DEAL with instead of HAVE. I truly think that when you start to see it as an annoyance it becomes easier to handle. BUT like I ALSO tell folks "FIND WHAT WORKS for YOUR PUZZLE" that I say is MS, since no 2 are alike and I have repeated this in my book and multiple blogs. Some things will work for 1 or 2 or 300, but it will not work for others. SO for me I CHOOSE to be happy and NOT stressed and NOT let MS get the best of me and my life EVEN when I was hospitalized for 2 months and in hospice for over a year. I knew I had to get up and be ME, with MS. BUT I choose to make it an insignificant issue rather than let it RUN my day to-day life.

Let me explain, I very well could have rolled over and just said things like "well it's over now", "I will NEVER WALK AGAIN, this is too hard", YES I also dealt with DEEP depression, but once again I CHOOSE to not let it get to me and did what I could. When it was suggested by the doctor to take an antidepressant, I checked for ways I could NATURALLY help myself. I tried 100's of ways; Meditation, Gardening, Pets, LONG walks. BUT for me it was a COMBO of GOD and DIET and helping others that brought me to NO MEDICATION AT ALL. NOW I must say I do feel BG-12 (Tecfidera) is a GOOD bet for me, so do not think that I believe my fight is over. THE fight is not over until we hear "A CURE FOR MS HAS BEEN FOUND" and it is coming but we must choose to not let the BS of MS destroy the HOPE we gain from ALL the WONDERFUL people we all come in contact with that help us LIFT our spirits and show us that MS can TRY but WE WILL WIN.

WE constantly ask WHY questions like "WHY is this happening to me"? "WHY don't I just get that procedure"? "WHY don't I walk as

GREAT as that person dealing with the same MS as ME"? …to name a few that I was asking myself after my 2009-10 relapse. Then I started asking the 'WHATS' not 'WHY's' and I starting feeling better because I changed those 'WHY'S' to WHAT I CAN POSSIBLY DO to turn this around; I found things like DR. Terry Wahls books on diet, Mr. Montel Williams on how to think positively also I read up on Dr. Mike Arata's work with CCSVI and noticed ONE common theme, ALSO I found this in the pages of the Bible which I try to stay involved with every day! IT'S A PERSONAL CHOICE and a journey. WE must ALL choose to take steps to do the correct things in OUR own lives. Notice I put it in all CAPITALS 'personal choice', I realized that I must choose if I want to just roll over and let MS win or FIGHT and make it tough for MS. Then something AMAZING happened, I regained 90% of my mobility back after being confined to a bed for 3 months relearning how to walk, talk and use my fine motor skills and even eat and control my bladder.

YES I wore a diaper... YES I had nurses wiping my back side... YES they were HELPING me from a wheelchair to the bed and back to the wheelchair. But then I started asking each trainer "what can I do by myself" instead of "WHY can't I...". I started to learn little things that I could do all on my own to help in my progress ALONG with my new knowledge about diet and life choices thanks to those doctors and TV personalities sharing how and what they did to help themselves and then shared with us. After WALKING out of a hospice, YES I still was using a walker, BUT it was too big for a bus so I had to reach deep down and say "what's stopping me from using just a cane"! Since I really had no choice or had to decide to spend MORE money to upgrade my bus ticket, I said "NO, the only thing stopping me is FEAR, I have come this far, NO need to stop now"! Now after 2 years in Las Vegas still doing the things I had to figure out I wrote about them in my BOOK and posted videos on my exercises on YouTube. I moved across the country ON MY OWN to the BEAUTIFUL city of Milwaukee.

I AM STILL working on NEW things to be doing and STILL asking WHAT instead of WHY and I am WALKING FURTHER and further than ever before in the heat AND the humidity. Yeah it bothers me, BUT it's 80% better ALL thanks to changing how I SEE and DEAL with MS. BUT NONE of this would be possible WITHOUT MY FAITH, FAITH to know I CAN and that I have the STRENGTH. SEE, for most of you, you NEVER thought of yourself as a quitter before MS, SO DON'T NOW, you are the same person as before just with a little or A LOT of challenges now. YOU can either float with the tide or SWIM with the fishes. I CHOOSE TO SWIM not just float and maybe get somewhere.

BUT SWIM and go somewhere!!! PLEASE DO NOT FLOAT!

Age and many other factors come into play when DEALING with MS. Like it takes the persons determination, faith, diet, ability to exercise and the WANT to do the basic things NECESSARY to fight back. NOW think on this… I am NOW 37, at the time of my 2nd relapse I was 31 and I was an ATHLETIC person. I was 5'10" and 320 lbs. at the time but for an OVER weight Hispanic I still could move along with the smaller guys NO PROBLEM. I know this HELPED me bounce back faster than say someone who might be 15+ years older and not as athletic as I was. SEE another thing that they should be telling us and researching is how the FACTOR of age and other medical issues will play a HUGE role in MS, fatigue and the ability to recover what from MS has taken.

FOR example, we know MS is making our body fight itself. SO, let's say the body is using 50% of its white blood cell army to fight itself AND then you're dealing with let's say an infection. NOW the body has to send 25% more to fight this, NOW you're at 75% of your body's NATURAL energy to fight those issues. NOW let's toss in normal body wear and tear due to age, energy to walk around OR just stay awake, move your legs, brain power, use of arms, hands, fingers and toes JUST to name a few. THIS ALL requires energy from your body at the same time your body is fighting things that are not NORMAL. EVEN your heart beat, lungs bringing IN and OUT air, EYE movement and THOUGHT processes require energy!

ALL of these things I have just mentioned require ENERGY from YOUR BODY, then we fill it with SO CALLED nutrients <junk food> that the body does not easily recognize and has almost

0% HELP to the white blood cells in our body. This, I believe is a MAJOR factor in the fatigue issue that no doubt MOST of us deal with, SO look into things that NATURALLY help the body to FIGHT. Remember the body has to work 2x harder to absorb things man-made, YES I am speaking about MEDICATION, YES we need it but understand it is a Band-Aid to take the PRESSURE off the body's NATURAL ways to heal itself. ALSO, in one of my other blogs I talked about how medication in 98% based off of a natural resource where it was found! IE: a plant. HMMMMMM, look to see what you're eating, it could be HARMING you WAY more than it is helping. There are CERTAIN foods the body is spending energy on JUST to recognize and also to try and digest. THEN where does it go? Does it HELP? OR HURT? Asking questions ONLY increases your OWN knowledge. BE your OWN advocate NO ONE knows YOU like YOU.

MS took many years to harm you, it took MANY tools to break you down, SO to believe there is 1 pill, or procedure or even a diet or an exercise to stop it WILL ALWAYS keep you in a state of depression or the "WOE IS ME" attitude as I call it. Understand, JUST because something worked for 'them' it MAY not work the same for you. Otherwise MS would not STILL be being diagnosed, WE would be saying "I HADDDDD" or as I say "I had DEALT WITH" MS and we would not be seeing MORE and MORE people with this HORRIBLE disease. See one of the 1st things I realized laying in my hospital bed unable to control most of my body was that it took 7 years from 2003 to 2010 to HIT me this hard. THEN I looked at ALL MS had taken from me; the ability to walk, eat on my own, the ability to use the restroom on my own let alone to control myself, FINE motor skills <to screw a nut on a bolt> and let's not forget the depressive times it brings forth.

SO to think there is going to be a PILL or a procedure that will take ALL this away is in my view insane, BUT medication with diet, with exercise and PMA <POSITIVE MENTAL ATTITUDE> are pieces to the PUZZLE called MS to start a GREAT way to fight back and regain some of the LOST comforts we once had. BUT as I wrote in my BOOK, we need to understand NO matter what, MS WILL fight us back. YOU will have GREAT DAYS and you will be reminded that you DEAL with something HORRIBLE every day.

I believe once we understand that this is more than a 'RIGHT NOW FIX disease' and start piecing together what works for us, the road MS has us walking on gets a little easier. BUT by no means think it is gone, JUST SMILE and say in YOUR HEART "I WON MS, I'm STILL HERE, I WILL NOT STOP, YOU MIGHT

THINK YOU HAVE ME BUT I DO NOT HAVE YOU, I just DEAL with your CRAP".

CHANGE THE OUTLOOK, IT CAN AND WILL CHANGE THE OUTCOME! We have PLENTY of GREAT teaching tools. Then we also know people who swear by the next get healed right now attitude, YOU know them they say stuff like "JUST GET UP AND WALK" or "YOU DO NOT LOOK SICK" or "BUT YESTERDAY YOU WERE FINE"... It never stops, BUT you ALSO have PIONEERS to show you it can be done like DR. Terry Wahls, Montel Williams, Jackie Joy, etc... THERE are 100's if not 1000's more I've had the pleasure of meeting, some on Facebook and some on Twitter. They ALL have THEIR stories and if you take the time to LISTEN you would hear stories of success but tangled in with their stories are tales of failure.

The issue they ALL have in common is THEY DID NOT QUIT and they KNEW there is NO ONE SIZE FITS ALL! <See the 3 pics of me on the back cover> See I found THE PIECES to MY PUZZLE and yes there were PLENTY of them and that day I wanted to quit OR I ASKED GOD for a 1 solution to this issue. I QUICKLY learned I had to FIGHT and to NEVER stop fighting because I NEVER knew what the next day would be like.

It took 4 years and LOTS of physical therapy, a GREAT healthy Dr. Wahls inspired diet, GREAT wisdom from MONTEL WILLIAMS, PRAYER, ALSO many days of falling, frustration, DEPRESSION and also feeling ALONE. BUT I remembered my SON and ALL those who did NOT have the opportunity I had with PT or OT and felt it would be a DISGRACE to just give up. BY knowing I had to PIECE things together renewed my mind and strength.

READING NOTES

CHAPTER 8

WHAT I USE TO MAKE ME STRONG IN MY MIND

I tend to look at life in a different manner than others, I play my own little short comedy film of how things go on in my mind, I found this not only helps reduce the stresses in life but allows me to get over a situation that has the potential to get under my skin and make me upset. I also do my best to hold dear to my Christian upbringing and faith now.

I know not everyone believes in GOD, but I do and it's the BIGGEST puzzle piece I have! So for those that are Agnostic, Atheist, Muslim, Jew or whatever things like being spiritual, DO what works for YOU. But I'm going to tell you things that I meditate on to help my mind be prepared for the battles of the day. See, we do not know what tomorrow holds so doing our best to letting go of things we cannot control is one of the best ways to ease stresses that you deal with on a day-to-day basis. Now if some of you are like me and are news junkies, well I know some of the ignorance we see gets us going, but that may be another book another day....

One of the first things I do every morning is pray, so some of you might meditate, some of you may make coffee and for those that can kiss your spouse or children PLEASE take a minute and see how LUCKY and BLESSED you are. I also hope to be back in this position BUT I use that HOPE to make me stronger today. To fight a little more, to take 1 more step when my legs are shaking because they feel like jello, to ignore those thoughts of "it's too tough" OR "I cannot", I just picture in my mind that day of getting up to walk to my son's bedroom and kiss his little forehead and make him and my spouse breakfast. These things I have to remind myself of hourly, when it seems like that storm will never break, when my rainbow is out BUT has no color, when I can see the blank, black sheet with no stars and NO moon, BUT I rejoice in the fact I am able to see the sky, that I am able to even see. We miss sooooooo much when we focus on things past and the as I call shoulda, woulda, coulda's in life, instead of seeing what's right there.

See the mere fact you are still alive to make a choice when you wake up, the mere fact someone CHOSE to stand by you in this storm OFTEN behind you holding the umbrella so YOU do not get wet while they freeze, proves that there are people who are willing to walk through this with you. Oh I know people walk away after they SWORE for many years to stand with you no matter what BUT if you look at that fine print it says 'as long as you're a winner in THEIR BOOK'. I have also had to slowly watch people fade away, YES, YES even family, BUT YOU'RE STILL HERE and you can make a difference for YOU. THINK "I AM THE ONLY PERON WHO CAN DO THIS FOR ME". YOU WILL keep remembering the pain in your mind and body shall pass but the toughness of your heart can and will NEVER leave you.

I also tend to remind myself of ALL those soldiers that come home after a life altering injury and made life work in their favor. I can just hear them in my mind saying "well NOW what, OK I'm built stronger than this, I can make this work, I have a wife/husband that's counting on me to pull it together, I am the best, I am strong". I asked myself what's the difference between them and me? NOTHING. I am also strong, I ALSO CAN DO THIS, then I press on when my mind says "QUIT". I watched the soldiers in Ft. Lewis of Tacoma, WA do what they call PT <PHYSICAL TRAINING> every morning when I worked there and I learned a few things; TRUE WARRIORS never give up, YOU can do 5 to 10% more after you think you're done, also its 90% in your head.

FEAR ~Now the Definition of fear-

1.fear Variation | Synonyms

Houghton Mifflin

n.noun A feeling of agitation and anxiety caused by the presence or imminence of danger.

A state or condition marked by this feeling. Living in fear

Fear and anxiety is something Multiple Sclerosis brings to us more often than not, SO knowing this gives you a daily head start knowing that this will be a part of the battle that lies ahead, it gives you the upper hand to prepare for it. So just remind yourself YOU CAN do it, it may be hard, one of the hardest battles to date in your life, just know this too shall pass.

YOU know I look back to a little over 3 years ago when I was living in a hospice and sharing a room with a gentleman over 60 years of age, just gives you an idea maybe of what I was looking at every day. ALSO there were 4 others at this home, 3 of which were also not expected to make it very much longer. The 4th was the live-in nurse and EVERY day I had to get up and have breakfast, sit in a room and watch TV with them, take meds and only dream of what my life used to be!

NOW, I am sitting in my home writing 3 books and a blog, doing interviews and helping my roommate overcome RRMS after she had been downgraded from SPMS and taken off her meds BY HER DOCTOR. NEVER do this on your own, ALWAYS CONSULT YOUR PHYSICIAN. I'M saying all this to show even at a time when YOU think it looks GRIM, NOTHING is going the way YOU thought, NO matter how far you run or drive the rain keeps falling, in most cases it gets harder and the light at the end of the road gets dimmer. Just remember EVERY step taken gets you CLOSER to getting out of that rain, ALSO if you take a moment to appreciate that, you will notice MANY who have driven or RAN in that SAME storm dropped UMBRELLAS to make things a LITTLE easier. JUST smile and say "HA, THIS IS ALL YOU GOT"? Look back and see for a MOMENT what you went through JUST before because this was giving you the strength to carry the load you have to carry now, BUT now it is raining to boot, so not only are you tired, weak, doubtful but YOU'RE also wet. Plenty of people have walked this road and left tools to help you in what I say is "the fight of our lives"

YOU can do it, YOU came through with just what was needed to make it through this. THIS is setting YOU up for what's next and that next MAY NOT BE THE finish line, but a finish line non-the-less so never stop believing that you CAN. This summer (June 2014) I'm headed to a book signing with a GIANT like DR. WAYNE DYER and other BEST selling authors that I feel SOOOOOO blessed to be in the presence of. SEE folks I had NO IDEA one little BOOK was formulating in my mind by the actions I dealt with by being stuck in a HOSPITAL bed, then a hospice, then 2 years in VEGAS, now I'm here in Milwaukee, WI on my own TRYING my best to help others, watching a woman who has had her body CRUSHED by SPMS for 20 years get to, after 4 years, WALK down the stairs to her basement, DRIVE HER OWN CAR, go from saying "RAY BEFORE YOU CAME I WAS PLANNING TO GO TO AN ASSISTED LIVING HOME" to now knowing she can do this on her OWN and WILL NOT have to live her life not being in control of it. BUT don't just think it was an easy road for her or me. Break through it! DO NOT be complacent with FEAR. REMEMBER your dreams because YOU can still achieve them. DOUBT is a tool FEAR uses when FEAR is FEARFUL of YOU!!!!

READING NOTES

CHAPTER 9

WAYS I HAVE KEPT MS AT BAY AND MY THOUGHTS

There was a time back in hospice when I woke up and laid in my room with my roommate snoring in the next bed realizing that they DID NOT tell me that there were a few things a person can do: 1. we can get depressed and give up! NO NOT ME, 2. You can ask the nurses for another room and get more comfortable. NO NOT ME, 3. YOU can TELL YOURSELF "I AM GOING

TO WALK OUT OF HERE AND LIVE MY
LIFE REGARDLESS OF WHAT MS AND
THE DOCTORS THINK", THIS WAS ME
and I know YOU have this thought also.

See, I decided at that point to give 10% more to
my diet, to try to be happy even in HOSPICE,
giving 10% more when using a walker in spite
of constant mind-numbing snoring from your
roommate because this was a hospice with 4
rooms and 2 women <over the age of 50 with
severe mental issues> and 3 guys <2 of which
were 60+> and then there was me in my early
30's. I then got up took 5 minutes to get my socks
on <I was still learning in occupational therapy>
grabbed my walker and headed to the restroom,
then I said <YUP, I"M GOING TO DO IT>
after I was dressed, brushed my teeth, dressed
and had breakfast taken care of, I headed for the
FRONT door. I was going to walk, YES walk

my handicapped buns down the road, not caring where I was going.

I had my cell phone JUST IN CASE I fell. SO I started walking down the driveway to the street. Now being in GRAHAM, WASHINGTON it was an area that had NO sidewalks. I had to push the walker OVER dirt, rocks and other things. NO easy task, let me tell you. So I would get maybe a quarter-mile when MS decides to rear the 'no energy' thing at me. YUP, YOU GUESSED it I FELL in the MIDDLE of NO WHERE! SIGHS, I felt defeated, BUT then I started to remember ALL THOSE SOLDIERS I would watch in Fort Lewis, NOW Lewis-McChord and I remember hearing the SEARGENT ALWAYS yelling "GIVE ME 10% MORE SOLDIER", SO I knew I could do more than what MS or those doctors TELL PEOPLE they can do. That's a MAJOR reason for me writing MY BOOK to inform people there is at least 10% MORE YOU

CAN DO that they do not inform you about. I mean, WOW why did it take the brilliance of DR. TERRY L. WAHLS to inform us about the wonders of DIET? ALSO Montel Williams to give us hope?

It is sad to see something as simple as a change in your diet and encouraging hope HELP SO MUCH! WELL it does and I see people that I told just a % of the things I had to do improve THEIR health. I AM SURE your fight if not HARDER, is difficult for you, KNOW even though I stopped my story at where I fell, I still had to head back! So after ALL that and a WHOLE lot more, I am here now in my home writing to you. After that day I had made a promise to myself to NOT EVER give up, to NEVER STOP, TO GIVE that 10% more even though it feels as though you can't. You can. NEVER STOP, you can do it, it is possible, dream again and it helps I KNOW.

This is something I know we ALL have felt, EVEN feel it now dealing with Multiple Sclerosis. I truly feel we are set up to fail! Let me explain. When we get diagnosed we are not told how we can beat and/or turn things around, so we are starting running backwards, making it HARDER to turn things around.

BUT do not fear no matter what STAGE THEY say you are in, YOU can start piecing together this giant of a puzzle we know as MS. Look at people like Dr. Terry L. Wahls, Montell Williams, EVEN non-stars like Jackie Joy who was recently DOWNGRADED from SPMS to RRMS and taken off 90% of her meds. DR. Wahls through her diet totally reversed her dealing with MS! Now these 3 are just a few examples of what can be done. Dr. Wahls with her BEAUTIFUL DIET, Jackie Joy using the principles used in my book and of course Montel Williams which, I'm sure if we did not have him ALOT of people would still be in the dark about MS.

OK, now when we look back it is only to try to gauge the progress we are currently making. NOW if you JUST fell into a relapse or flare-up or whatever we call it, then we will say that is a starting point. NOW this is what I mean, MOST people get disappointed when they took 4 steps yesterday and ONLY took 3 steps today. OK, so people only notice the 1 less step they did NOT take, WELL I SAY concentrate on the 3 steps that you did… it's better than have taken ZER0… SEE 1/2 is more than ZERO, so it is a positive. But then we make excuses like "WELL BEFORE I COULD RUN A MILE" and unfortunately we use our past as a progress meter as to how we should be now.

OK TIME FOR SOME HARD TRUTH! YOU ARE NOT THAT PERSON NOW, <body wise>

but we forget to bring our minds into the present. LOOK we DEAL with MS and now we need not only to start living healthier to help our bodies to fight it, BUT we also need to sling shot our minds to the here and now to understand we have to look at the wins and progresses in a different matter. JUST remember 1/2 is more than ZER0. One step is your 1st step in a direction you want to go. FORWARD PROGRESS starts with a step in A DIRECTION. REMEMBER, we can only go FORWARD in time, YOU can look back, but use it to SMILE, a teaching method or inspiration, NEVER use it as a basis to beat yourself down or compare to how you were <BEFORE MS>. You're just setting yourself up for disappointments

How do you feel? In my case I felt ALONE, which in turn made me depressed. See I have not told many people about how or what happened RIGHT before my relapse and then into my relapse and then the hospital days...

Well, I will FINALLY tell you guys so when you read this it's just not ANOTHER person trying to say "YA, I UNDERSTAND" but has NO knowledge on how MS takes and takes!!

OK, December of 2009, I do not remember the date all I know is it was another Sunday morning and I was getting ready for church. See, I had to walk there due to the fact my live-in girlfriend left me with our son 3 months earlier but I had to be thankful, at least I was able to see him once a week. SO back to it, I got ready, walked out of my front door, locked it, walked 2 steps then fell backwards hitting my head on the door and my body went LIMP. I am not sure how long I laid there but when my next door neighbor found me and took me back inside to my bed AFTER I had been pleading with him not to call 911 and that I was OK, it was 2 hours later so I assume and tell folks it was 2 hours.

The next day I was still not able to control ANY part of my body. When I had a NEED, you know the one that tells you 'HEY BUDDY, UMM BATHROOM'?, so with everything I could I attempted to get to my restroom and I somehow got there and got to the sink but well when it was time to go it was time to go, so I flung myself in the direction of the toilet and ALMOST made it but to no avail, I missed, I fell between the toilet and the tub. OK, now I notice I have gained SOME of my strength back BUT now I am between the toilet and the tub and I'm no small guy, I'm 5' 10" and 300+ lbs. at the time of this event so I called 911... OK OK OK enough of that let's get to me at the hospital with about 20% control of my UPPER body extremities. BUT I cannot walk and have NO control over the volume of my voice. I had no idea as to what's going on because for the last 6 years I was in what they call a REMISSION.

You see, the doctor who diagnosed me did not explain what was next or what I could do to combat this or that a REMISSION was possible so I was clueless. OK, in the hospital I had to go through a series of tests for them to figure this out; MRI's, a spinal tap, blood tests, etc. SO once it was found to be MS AGAIN I was admitted to a rehab floor where I had to RELEARN how to walk, use my voice, relearn motor skills, EVEN how to use the restroom. YES people, as a man I was shown how men pee and for 7 months I needed a nurse to wipe my backside! EVERY morning at 6 am an OT came in to make sure I was getting dressed, that I had brushed my teeth and then sat with me during breakfast to make sure I did not CHOKE on my food and DIE.

BUT EVERY MORNING I had to look in a mirror and it seemed to NEVER look back! VERY depressing. See I was looking in that mirror for the person I WAS, not who I had become to

FIGHT this MONSTER we know as Multiple Sclerosis. OR the person I became BECAUSE of the MONSTER MS!!

We ALL have looked into that mirror and it does not look back. For some it is getting older, some believe they are ugly, some for some reason hate themselves. BUT for me it was ALL that AND dealing now with MS! The thought of now I HAVE to have someone wipe my backside that is 5 to 10 years my junior!? I AM 31 YEARS OLD, I told myself YOU'RE A MAN, HOW CAN YOU LET SOMEONE TELL YOU HOW TO PEE LIKE A MAN? HOW COME YOU CANNOT WALK? WHERE IS YOUR SON? NO ONE WILL EVER LOVE YOU NOW. WHERE'S YOUR FAMILY? YOU'RE ALL ALONE LOSER! My mind was haunting me, this is what the man in the mirror was telling me. At this point I DECIDED to FIGHT. I was VERY OBSERVANT to the diet being fed to me in the hospital and also asking questions. I also would watch EVERY move the physical therapist would make to see IF I could somehow do this on my own. SO, after 4 to 6 months I was moved to a hospice. I did out-patient therapy for 2 months afterward but I would continue to try to figure out ways to do some of those therapies at the hospice. I would ask the therapist how to do this at the hospice, after a few months I started to walk with a walker.

ALL of this until now I was VERY EMBARRASSED to talk about because when I looked into the mirror I WANTED to see the guy who used to weight lift, who was a FOREMAN for the demolition team, who could wipe his own back side! BUT, I know this is the same man only now with NEW CHALLENGES. So after 5 years now I have control of 95% of my body and live on my own and figured out how to BEAT and KEEP ON beating this monster called MS by putting the pieces in the mirror together again. THE picture I see is now one of a FUTURE, NOT OF WHAT I WAS <sick>!!! Make the choice to NOT GIVE UP. PUT the PIECES of your mirror together like a puzzle. BUT this time see what YOU'RE GOING to do not what you have done before, ONLY look back as a reference to either remember the GOOD times to keep the depression monster at bay!

READING NOTES

CHAPTER 10

LOOKING FORWARD

In this chapter we will talk about looking forward. I don't look back, ever. Look forward in noticing the small things that we do. Not the big picture. Your focus going forward will be to notice all the little "wins". When you take a half step forward, it's a win. It's better than to not take any steps at all. You want to think about walking and imagine walking. Dream about walking. Remember what it feels like to go on a long walk. This exercise will set up your brain and your cells for walking.

Because this is going to keep you forward-looking in what you should be accomplishing. Don't settle for nothing (NO-thing). Always dream and vision something positive, move forward, imagine yourself moving forward, be all that you want to be, do the things you need to do to get to that spot. Don't accept the norm, what MS or what your doctor says MS should be. As a good friend put it, don't be the status quo! You can do more than what you think you can and if you're tired of hurting and you're in pain, remember the body can do 5%-10% more. If you don't believe me watch a show like "Surviving the Cut" or any video for our Special Forces. Watch recruits who are pushed to their limits and then do 5%-10% MORE! The human body is resilient. This will show you how far they push their bodies, therefore you can push your body too. But please know and understand your body is dealing with MS. Please see yourself doing what you want to be doing not what you were doing. Remember you're going forward not backwards. So stop saying what should have been or what I was or what I did in the past and start saying what I'm going to do, what I am and what I'm becoming. This is how I live every day. I tell myself I'm going to do this today and then I will do more tomorrow. See yourself doing this. Motivate yourself to do this. Become what you dream, dream what you will become. The choice is yours!

In other chapters you'll notice that I say to look forward to be forward. The small wins will help you stay motivated to look forward and you will have bad days. Just don't get down, remember you will win. Keep this in mind at all times. None of this will be easy. But, it will be worth it. Like they say, "we can build it again; it will be built a bit better".

Understand do not look at what you were, but look to where you want to be. You will be better, keep that in mind, if you keep looking at where you were you will never get to where you want to be. Remember I said a half a step is better than no steps at all. Have you tried walking forward while looking backwards? You tend to run into things. Does that seem like the problem we face with MS? We're always worried about what we were and how we're going get back to our old self, not knowing we are being built to be a better version of who we were.

READING NOTES

CHAPTER 11

CHOICE

Now we all have choices to make and I have made the choice to look for the good in dealing with MS rather than being negative. Now I know this is not everyone's cup of coffee. I know some think I'm being crazy and that I'm in denial, WELL denial as they call it led me out of a hospital and a hospice to move from Washington State to Las Vegas with family to eventually in my own place for rent… ALL while I was doing my own rehab with whatever I could find.

I took walks around my block knowing I might get laughed at for the way I walk because it was like trying to walk on a water bed. LOL, but I made the choice to smile rather than worry about what others might think. We all go through stuff, it's the ones who can smile and chuckle during those times that press onward. SO please make a choice and a commitment to yourself to press on and find <as I call> the FUNNY in things that would otherwise break someone else down! Remember, most do not understand MS or even know about it, so what we show them is how it may affect their day and what THEY are going through.

People at 1st will not get it but they eventually will, case in point; most of us WILL NEVER know what it's like to be a soldier and suffer from WAR PTSD but our hearts go out to them because we know that the pain they have to deal with is almost unbearable. BUT most push through showing us what strength REALLY is, SO show MS you are ALSO a soldier in the MS war and carry the same type of bravery and resolve to press onward and to never quit. Make that choice and be that brave, in this show YOUR mind, body and YOUR soul that YOU control it not MS. I can remember when I had hardly ANY control over my body and I did have control over my mind BUT it was being bombarded with attacks of thoughts like "give up, you're never going to be the same. YOU'RE a loser just roll over and quit, where are your friends, where is your son, where is your girlfriend, they all promised they got you and where are they now? SEE you're not worth it". These are a few thoughts I had to deal with as I stared up at that ceiling or at the blood pressure machine every night beeping and while a nurse 10 years younger wiped my backside because I lacked the coordination to do it myself. Now through ALL of this I finally said "ENOUGH MS, I can and WILL beat you"! Not knowing how, but I choose at that point not to give up. I thought back to my parents and all they had to go through, many do not know I was adopted at 2 days old by an African American family, my mother and father were from the south born in 1927. SO if you know your history <I'M A HISTORY NUT> they did not even have the right to vote until 1968 and still to this day in 2014 we deal with racism, it's just hooded different. My parents made it through ALL that AND the Great Depression and still had 7 children AFTER 1 drown in a lake in Illinois plus my father was a VERY successful Pastor and my mother is still with us at 87 <at the time of this writing> I thought to myself "There is NO WAY I'm going to allow MS to destroy ALL that GOD has built in me", SO I fought and FOUGHT, yeah I lost battles BUT I'm going to win the war.

Now I am in Milwaukee living on my own, HAPPY and still fighting the fight against MS.

YES, MS still wins battles but like I said I WILL win the war. I walk over a mile to the store each week in the humidity and in snow after I was told this could never happen <ME WALKING>. Every year I WALK to the state fair and enjoy deep fried EVERYTHING they offer LOL. I get to enjoy all the farm animals and shop at my own LEISURE. SO earlier I told you people will say that I am in denial, OK I'll be in denial like they say and while they are saying it I am still WALKING, SHOPPING, LIVING ON My OWN, writing books, traveling the USA, meeting GREAT PEOPLE all on my own. SO if this is denial OK THEN, BRING me MORE!!! Make your choice!!!

READING NOTES

CHAPTER 12

WHERE I FOUND SUPPORT

There are many ways to find support. There are places like Facebook and Twitter that I have found and I'm sure if you call you NMSS <National Multiple Sclerosis Society>, they can get you some info on places that meet. I have joined MANY groups on Facebook and even made my own group on Facebook, Twitter and Google +. There is also Instagram, Linkden and Pinterest. I found by sharing my pieces to this puzzle that it not only helped others but helped me in return. I have gained SOOO much creating a place where people can go to chat on what HELPS and are not always talking about the negatives. I felt as though in almost every group I visited it was just complain, complain and complain but not give 1 helpful response or even a suggestion......

Well, so I decided to make a group on Facebook called "NO MORE MS DEPRESSION" with over 2400+ members. Not only do we 98% of the time try to focus on what is helping OR finding pieces to OUR own puzzle that has helped but we are there to LIFT up anyone who at ANY time is down. WE all understand that it's not all unicorns and rainbows dealing with MS. I do also know that people need to vent, YES get it off your mind, just to make a home there or even camp there, it's now just a downward spiral into depression the more we focus on the negatives.

I also found that for me just getting out to a mall or a store helps to be around people. I know this is not easy for everyone. I know what it is like to be confined to a bed or stuck in a hospice unable to move until someone lifts you out of your bed and places you in your wheelchair and has to push you into the restroom only to have them brush your teeth and help you use the restroom. <YES, HELP YOU AS A MAN USE THE RESTROOM>. OH, I KNOW, so once you have the ability to do this, PLEASE do so because it helps reawaken your mind into realizing you're NOT trapped in a lonely existence and it awakens those cells in your body. Humans are not made to be lonely beings. So just being out and about in some sort of cellular way makes your body jump for joy, it's the best ANTIDEPRESSANT I have found for me at least.

ALSO learn to forgive YOURSELF first of all and get around family <if they help you even if they do not> the reason I say this is because sometimes people lash out at what they fear and the only way they know how to react is to be negative towards you. NOW know this, it is not YOUR fault, it's probably not theirs either. JUST know some who do not understand Multiple Sclerosis will lash out at you for dealing with it, just remember YOU are the only teacher they are going to have, SO if you lash back it just makes them RIGHT <in their minds> in that they need to stay away and put more of a wedge between them and you. BUT if you show them that you are the SAME or even a better person even dealing with Multiple Sclerosis not only can you win their heart but help teach that person how just because life was unfair, people can and WILL be ok and have peace in a time of all out anarchy. This in turn will help YOU see that you are a better person because of Multiple Sclerosis and Multiple Sclerosis will lose a vital grip in the war we deal with day to day.

See now YOU have become the one person support group you have been looking for, EVERYONE is and WILL wonder how a person like you who has

EVERY reason to quit, IS NOT quitting. I have a few people because of Multiple Sclerosis that I have met and a few before Multiple Sclerosis. They have TOUCHED my heart and I'M going to name them, I usually do not do this but they to me are worth it; Jackie E Joy, Rae Markable Edwards, Judi Leqoc, Jamie Deannette Reaves, Noah Reaves, Hannah and Landon Reaves. ALSO if you know me and have read my 1st book you will know I WILL ALWAYS turn to my SON Christian Rey Taijeron Garcia for a smile and inspiration and I thank GOD for this gift! These are my internal support group, JUST to name a few and there are A LOT more, I would need an entire BOOK just to name them....

See support groups come in the way you find them and in your own mind. I pray you shake yourself loose of the chains Multiple Sclerosis tries to put you in, also if you cannot find a group you like then know you can make you own!

READING NOTES

CHAPTER 13

ADVANCED MEDICINE

When we think of medication we think of Tysabri, Copaxone, Rebif, Betaseron, Tecfidera, etc., WELL I think of outpatient services like occupational therapy, physical therapy, CCSVI, stem cells, etc. These are ALL things that COULD be an important piece to YOUR puzzle. ALSO I think of groups like those either on Facebook or in person or just someone you can talk with. Never underestimate these, for the mental boost from just chatting with someone is a MAJOR WIN in my book. Make sure you can find someone who can help you get outside and to be around people and out in the sun to get NATURAL VITAMIN D. There are MANY studies as to the BOOST it gives our bodies. And there are many things they are figuring out like ALSO just being around others helps your mind realize that you are not alone, it stops the feeling, in a way that the walls are closing in and you get to see the beauty of the world. To some this may not help, so like I ALWAYS say "do what's best for you".

Always heed advice EVEN if at that moment it does NOT apply to you. I say this because if it does not help now it could in your future OR it will show you what NOT to do. ALSO now they have FINALLY and officially said that being active may be good for you, as I said in my last book **No More MS Depression 101** that exercise helps blood flow, wakes up the MUSCLES that may have atrophied, gets the blood flowing which means oxygen COURSING throughout the areas of the body that may be screaming for it and it has a HOST of other BENEFITS. NOW PLEASE CONSULT your DOCTOR on this because for some it may hurt and some it will HELP. It's YOUR body not mine or his or hers or EVEN the doctors, SO please find your piece to the puzzle that makes your picture a little more clear.

READING NOTES

CHAPTER 14

ADVANCED EXERCISE

We all need to try to start seeing what our body responds to for not ALL exercises helps, A LOT might cause extra strain to areas that are ALREADY trying to heal on their own but since we think it is not fast enough, we make it a priority in our work out which can reverse what the body is doing. Now let me explain what I mean, at the gym there is NO need to do SUPER leg exercises when you ALREADY walked just to get to the leg workout machine. I have this theory that YOU burn at least 3x the amount of energy as someone who does NOT deal with MS. SO knowing this, just walking you would have burned and exerted 3x the energy and muscle strength to get to the machine OR the area to work out those SAME leg muscles WHEN you can use the PRECIOUS little energy we get to work on let's say CORE muscles. If you have done your research on balance then you KNOW this is a VITAL part of standing and walking straight.

See, many times I went to the gym and worked on my legs thinking I was helping them. BUT I started to notice that I was getting tired before I got to the hip flexor machine and could only do half as many reps as I would have liked to do. So one day I decided to do my leg work out LAST instead of first in my rotation and I was able to do more reps in other areas and noticed my legs still felt tired from JUST walking back and forth to each machine.

Now I know some of you are thinking "WELL, I do not have a GYM membership", this is ok. Like I have shown in my videos on YouTube as to how to use YOUR basic home items to work out as though you're at a GYM. Take note of how far you walk just from your bed when you walk to your restroom, to the kitchen, back to your area that you watch TV, then you have to get up and WHILE standing exert energy to make yourself lunch or a snack then walk back. THEN add how many times you have to get UP <this is what I consider a minor SQUAT using NATURAL BODY WEIGHT> and ALL these things whether you see it or not is exercise. REMEMBER my theory of burning AT LEAST 3x the amount of energy as someone who does NOT deal with MS.

NOW try a few things while you're waiting on your microwave to reheat the VEGGIES <WINK WINK> you had for dinner last night; just grab the counter with both hands spread like you going to do a push up and knock out 5 to 10 before your food heats up or PUT both hands on the counter SAFELY and make sure you're stable, close your eyes and feel your body try to find center. ALL which, JUST standing there, you are BURNING at least 3x the amount of energy as a person who does not deal with MS. See, when I was first diagnosed, like MANY OF you I was told to "take it easy, DO NOT overdue it". THIS is true, NEVER go beyond your OWN energy store for YOUR BODY, ONLY you know when that is BUT we are ALL treated as people dealing with Multiple Sclerosis should NOT do anything that exerts energy therefore leading us to the development of MORE muscle atrophy. BUT to me this made NO sense. Why would a DOCTOR tell me to take it easy YET my PHYSICAL therapist, I SWEAR was attempting to kill me with learning to walk again, always telling me "JUST A FEW MORE YARDS,

RAY"!, then it felt like 5 miles, OR just 2 more minutes on the arm machine BUT she leaves and comes back 15 minutes later..... Hmmmm, how is it that one DOCTOR is saying DON'T exert yourself yet the person who works with the issues of PHYSICAL THERAPY tells me to do MORE?? SO, I decided to Google this and I read that probably 1/2 said exercising was OK for US and 1/4 said NO it's bad to do this and 1/4 was still waiting on the research findings from people who are TRAINED in PHYSICAL THERAPY. See, I saw that FOR ME I needed to find my stopping point and not overexert myself, just work out RIGHT to that point and rest and take note as to how long of a rest was needed to be able to do more. OH YES and also I did notice WE CAN GET OUR ENERGY back again, it just takes longer, SOMETIMES A LOT longer but we do. SO all in all, SEE how this will work for YOU and YOUR life DEALING with MS and remember QUESTION EVERYTHING for when YOU see YOUR limits YOU then will see how YOUR body can respond to how MS affects YOU.

I work with my roommate Jackie Joy, who dealt with SPMS and was recently downgraded to RRMS <WHICH IS A RARE THING to happen>. I told her to start using a walker again rather than the wall walking thing, let me explain why. WHEN you wall walk, YES it seems as though you're getting around like you used to but you JUST need that LITTLE extra balance. TO ME this is FALSE HOPE, your PRIDE seems to keep you looking back as to how others may perceive you with a walker OR you tell yourself "I DON'T NEED IT, I'M NOT DISABLED". FUNNY, YOU tell YOU this and this is what YOU think others see. BUT when you use a wall you are not RETRAINING the muscles needed to walk, you are making the brain think YOU just need to LEAN instead of forcing the brain to train the muscles needed to walk the way the body was intended <up-right>. It's like trying to ride a bike RELEARNING the balance aspect BUT you go and put training wheels on the back but then also on the front... with the walker Jackie noticed there were muscles in her legs that started to strain that she had NOT felt in YEARS! YOU see, the MUSCLES are starting to reactivate that are vital to walking and/or balance. I also noticed that she was standing A LOT straighter with less sway. SEE, if you'll JUST stand in place or sit and close your eyes, put each hand out to the side and notice your MIND trying to figure where center is, I call this CELL muscle memory. Jackie, by now using the walker instead of wall walking is retraining her muscles and brain to unlock what her brain ALREADY knew but MS had severed the connections that were needed to make happen. BUT by doing the simple task of using a walker INSTEAD of the wall, that simple modification FORCED her brain to make NEW connections. BUT remember things in your body need time to GROW and you must help it get stronger by working that area out.

ONE thing I did a lot was take some OLD milk 1 gallon containers and fill them with water and do curls and dead lifts to build my arm and leg strength and core-type exercises. Also I would invest in resistance bands as there is a WIDE range of things to be done with them and they are VERY cheap at Amazon, Kmart, Walmart, etc. Start working on the areas YOU need. I can ONLY say the things I have dealt with on my journey which is by NO means done. It's been 4 years and I'm still working on things. ONLY you, not a BOOK, not a DOCTOR, friend or even family member can tell YOU how or what you feel. REMEMBER you make the choice to not eat well, YOU make the choice to not exercise or for 2 minutes to get those bands and knock out 2 reps of 25 curls or windmills to strengthen YOUR arms or chest. SO let's not complain that it's too hard now, WHEN YOU can make the CHOICE to fit the EXERCISE PUZZLE PIECE in but YOU choose not to!

Using a pool is great therapy for MS, not only does it make you almost weightless but it allows you the confidence of knowing if you happen to lose balance you won't hurt yourself. Also, I found the resistance that the water provides helps in rebuilding muscles with extreme atrophy, even the muscles that are not commonly known. I would spend about 1 to 2 hours daily every week for 7 months in my cousin's pool in Las Vegas and do things like walk forward and then backwards, also side to side, after this I would do the same near a ledge with my eyes closed to FORCE the brain to then rely on my other senses. If you look it up, it takes more than your eyes to walk, you also need touch and your ears, so by closing my eyes it forces the brain to rely on other senses and your brain should remember this when your eyes are open to help walking then.

This is what I refer to as muscle and brain memory. See, those connections either are broken or misfiring and by doing this your body will make new connections, BUT know this takes time. Remember it took months or even years for MS to break up those connections so expect months at least to renew them.

READING NOTES

_____

_____

_____

_____

_____

_____

_____

_____

_____

_____

_____

_____

_____

_____

_____

CHAPTER 15

DEXTERITY

I used this also in my blog at Ramonhyrongarcia.com

It is one of the MANY things when dealing with MS to go! But I have researched and have found some doctors use Video Games to help patients with their concentration and steadiness of hands… SO I got to thinking "I am an AVID gamer… how can this help my issues with control, steadiness and concentration???" I then started paying attention to ALL the online games that I play in how it might benefit me with my recovery dealing with MS. I noticed not only was I having to concentrate on where I was going (in the game) but I had to remember things like what 'spell' to use when and how to get back to home base… NOW whether playing a game with a controller or using a mouse and keyboard you are looking at the screen and having to move your hands ALL AT ONCE. Now this is a form of what I call MUSCLE and CELL memory. Multitasking, I believe and study after study proves this, here are a few…

http://www.livestrong.com/article/175954-multitasking-activities-for-brain-injury-rehabilitation/,

http://www.ninds.nih.gov/news_and_events/news_articles/pressrelease_prefrontal_cortex_051299.htm, and last

http://lifehacker.com/5922453/
what-multitasking-does-to-our-brains...

These are a few web sites that talk about multitasking and how it helps. I WILL have an EXTENSIVE look on dexterity and OTHER things I have used to help me regain 95% of what MS took... but here is how I started, in my 1st BOOK I show the MANY ways I started to eventually BEAT DOWN MS and regain my life back.

As many of you have already noticed Yoga has been a HUGE factor in MANY of the rehabilitation methods used and Physical Therapy is one of the greatest tools that will need to be used at 1st to combat the issues that may be present with a MS patient. We will need to start fighting this right when we know for sure as to the diagnosis. Doctors and medical professionals need to start making us aware of the many benefits of keeping yourself active and dexterous and also how it will increase the blood flow WHICH in turn gets oxygen moving throughout the body. BUT also making the patients aware of how much to do, when the best time is to stop and HOPEFULLY good diet habits to go along with all this!

READING NOTES

CHAPTER 16

MOVE

In this chapter I will talk about always moving. Do not stand still. If something is in the way, find a way around it. I know this sounds easier said than is done, but what I really mean is if there's a roadblock you will find a way around it. Look at MS as a roadblock. I know it's hard to walk, if you can walk at all, if you're in a chair do leg exercises. Just never stop moving!

Everything boils down to a choice. Don't just sit there and say 'woe is me'... do what you need to do to get where you need to get. Back when I was in the hospice in a wheelchair, I just gave up, threw my hands up and said forget it. This is too hard. This is what I mean by keeping a positive mental attitude, always know that if you're breathing you're alive and you can do it!

MS tries to make you think you can't. I don't allow it and you should not allow other things and people to tell you what you can do and are capable of. Now when people run miles, remember every step of that long mile gets you closer to the end. But then you need to choose, is this the end? You can either stop there or go further.

Same issue I dealt with when I was in a wheelchair, just sit there and roll and learn to live, or get up and work as hard as I could. I didn't allow others to hold me back and you should not allow others to dictate your life's story. Find your motivation to keep moving no matter what.

I heard Pastor T.D. Jakes say even if he was in a bed, he would move his arms and he would kick his legs, he would never stop moving. This is the same attitude everyone should have when it comes to gaining their life back. Never give up, is your life really that important to you? Then why would you just roll over and fall for the status quo.

The medical field would have me believe at the time of my relapse, that I would never walk. They even sent me to a hospice and called it an adult family home. When I finally realized this was a place that they sent you when they figured you would not make it, I made up my mind to not sit still, I made up my mind to fight, to not believe what others say and to believe what my spirit was saying.

READING NOTES

CHAPTER 17

THE PUZZLE

By Jackie E. Joy

The concept explained in this chapter is so vital that I introduced it in the first book MS-101 and then continued to expand on it in this book, MS-102.

When Ramon began mentoring me to help me deal with MS, he taught me the concept of the puzzle. It all made sense right away. I got it, it was very clear. MS is so very different for everyone yet we are all placed into the same buckets, there's one entitled relapsing remitting, there's one entitled secondary progressive, there is one entitled primary progressive and now there's rumor of additional buckets.

In MS research for over 100 years it has been known that MS produces lesions in the brain and often on the spinal cord. The interruption of nerve signals coming from those areas produces most of the symptoms. I am resisting saying that it causes all of the symptoms because I really don't know. I do know that depending on which areas there is a lesion that will determine where on the body symptoms exist. I can also tell you from personal experience that your brain tries very hard to work with those interrupted signals. In the beginning years of my diagnosis I experienced poor circulation and poor sensory signals in my feet. I discovered this one day in the shower. I was using a handheld shower and I held it so that the water sprayed away from me because I had the hot water turned on and was waiting for it to warm up. Very cold water flowed on the shower floor but I couldn't tell if it was cold or hot. The water quickly warmed up and still I couldn't tell if it was cold or hot. I realized there was temperature but my brain seemed confused as to whether it was a hot sensation or a cold sensation. From this incidence I realized that due to an interrupted signal coming through nerves with a damaged myelin sheath, the brain would be capable of misunderstanding that signal. When I hear other patients explain things like pins and needles, numbness or pain, I often wonder if sometimes it is due to an interrupted signal coming through nerves with a damaged myelin sheath. In the early days after diagnosis I experienced patches of numbness on my legs. I feel very blessed to report that the numbness totally healed. It has not been back since. I can also tell you that I continued working for 20 years after diagnosis. In my mind these two things have a connection.

I have only been working on my puzzle (dealing with MS) for a year as far as this concept goes. In my first year, with Ramon's help, I've found that exercise is beneficial and that my body seems to quicker degrade when I slack off. I believe that due to the interrupted signals coming through nerves with a damaged myelin sheath exercise is harder for an MS patient but the benefits are greater because not only are we rebuilding strength but new pathways are being created and where possible, damaged pathways are being repaired. At a cellular level, for us, there is a lot more happening then in the body of a person who is not dealing with MS or any other debilitating issue. Ramon has helped me to understand that coming back from dealing with MS is truly a mind, body and spiritual connection. In the summer of 2014 I underwent eye surgery (recovery was 100%, I am delighted to report) and although I faced six weeks of recovery where I was instructed not to exert myself, I learned something important about healing and about my body specifically. During six weeks of recovery I did not exercise. I followed my doctors' instructions. Anybody else would have been frightened over this, but I had the benefit of conferring with Ramon during this process. He helped me to understand that my body was putting energy into healing my eye and now there was little or no energy for other areas. I made this information a tool to put in my toolbox. When I'm doing well, feeling well and I've slept well I know that I will receive maximum benefits from the energy that I invest in exercise. On days (there are less and less) when I'm not doing well I'll exercise lightly and not stress over it. There is always tomorrow. Working WITH my body and not AGAINST my body is a new concept for me. I hear people say they are "fighting" something, whether it's excess weight or weight in the wrong places or even bad hair. I've seen more benefit in my own body this past year by changing my attitude regarding working "with" my body rather than "fighting". When I was released to start exercising again, don't get me wrong, losses were not regained overnight. But it went much quicker than I expected. I lost nothing and the six weeks that I gave my body a chance to heal correctly produced excellent results.

Diet is another piece to my puzzle and honestly I can't imagine how it could not be a piece to everyone's puzzle. By following Dr. Terry Wahl's, I discovered that I am gluten sensitive and dairy contributed in a big way to the fatigue that I was dealing with. I did a lot of my own research on Google on GMO's, pesticides, the benefits of organic food, preservatives and vitamins. Dr. Wahl's books on the Paleo diet are the best I've ever read and should be in your toolbox. There is wisdom and knowledge in her books that is unparalleled. Anyone can take her book and start taking the necessary steps to clean up your diet, make the right choices at the market and figure out what needs to be added and removed to enable your body to be nourished and healed. Hippocrates who is the father of Western medicine said to let medicine be your food and your food to be medicine to your body. When doctors graduate and go on to practice medicine they take the "Hippocratic oath" which is based on Hippocrates. Does anyone else hear the oxymoron here? (Do not get me started)

PMA (positive mental attitude) connects the mind and the body. How do I know this? Because the opposite is also true, a negative mental attitude affects blood pressure, heart rhythm, adrenaline, hormones, blood flow including circulation and chemicals. When I mentioned chemicals I'm speaking of the chemical balance that is naturally present in our bodies. Cells are communicating with each other every day, all day and all night. When people meditate it slows down heart and respiration. When your friend tells you that you have a spider on your shoulder, even though you can't see it, your respiration and heartbeat increases. When you watch a scary movie your heartbeat and respiration increases in anticipation. All these changes within your body result from thoughts. When the telephone rings in the middle of the night it changes your heartbeat and respiration. The above-mentioned changes in heartbeat and respiration are all due to outside influences. No one and nothing need touch you. Your body changed the way it was operating simply by thoughts, by anticipation. PMA works like this in reverse. Expect the best, see it in your mind, reach for it and work for it and so your cells start the process of communicating with each other to bring it to pass. You have probably heard that "stress is a killer", well it is. Most everyone that I have spoken to dealing with MS can cite traumatizing events that preceded the first attack. Most everyone can also tell you that stress causes them to have trouble sleeping, have trouble walking and trouble functioning in general. Albert Einstein said "Everything is energy and that's all there is to it. Match the frequency of the reality you want and you cannot help but get that reality. It can be no other way. This is not philosophy this is physics". But, as a Christian I prefer to heed what Jesus said "For verily I say to you, that whoever shall say to this mountain, Be thou removed, and be thou cast into the sea; and shall not doubt in his heart, but shall believe that the things which he saith shall come to pass; he shall have whatever he saith." Whether you are God-fearing or Atheist it is how everything is made. A PMA positively affects your cells and your body. NMA (negative mental attitude) fuels stress, increases heartbeat and respiration, causes the adrenal gland to secrete hormones (necessary for flight or fight), contributes to body aches and headaches, upsets your stomach, plays havoc with your digestive system especially the colon, may or may not induce a skin response (rash, hives, goose bumps, sweating), etc. etc. When your adrenaline gland secretes adrenaline in response to stress and the stress does not exist the excess adrenaline in your bloodstream is responsible for health problems. Do you not see the power that exists in negativity? Turn this around and now you see the potential power in positivity, namely PMA.

READING NOTES

CHAPTER 18

BABY STEPS, BABY

By Jackie E. Joy

Before you start this chapter I would like you to consider reading the chapter entitled THE PUZZLE. Understanding the concept of MS as being a puzzle is vital in your journey. Whether you read it now or later, you'll find 'THE PUZZLE' referred to numerous times in this book and the first book MS-101.

In thinking back, it feels as though MS was trying to enter my life early on. I chose this title for my biography because I've always felt that MS had entered my life in baby steps (little by little) and I've been dealing with it ever since in baby steps (slowly but surely).

As a child, the heat of summer was especially hard on me. During summer vacation I slept until noon almost every day of the week. Even as a child, I knew that something was not right. In the early morning hours I could hear my friends laughing and playing outside. I was still in bed. Exhausted. The summer heat took its toll on me every day. When I misbehaved and was punished, the stress would weigh so heavily on me that it would drive me up to my bedroom to take a nap. Not just for an hour or two, but four or five hours. If I got hurt or cut myself it produced stress also and again it was nap time for the next 4 to 5 hours. Even as a child I knew something was different. I knew my friends and my siblings were not dealing with the things that I was and

I assumed that one day in the future it would all become clear.

Another issue that I now recognize as 'different' was that I could never listen to music (or TV) and study. All my friends listened to music while studying, but for me my brain couldn't do both.

Sleeping too much for me, continued into my teens and beyond until I received the diagnosis of MS. Prior to the diagnosis I suffered a month long episode of complete numbness on my right side from head to toe which could never be explained. During that period, needless to say, I underwent a myriad of tests at the local hospital. Several years following this episode I was stricken with optic neuritis at work. I need to interject an observation at this point; during both of these episodes even though they were five or six years apart, they both occurred during times in my life when I was under extreme stress. Without going into the details of the stress I was under, the point is that I hear other people dealing with MS recall moments of extreme stress in their lives that precede the diagnosis and the symptoms of MS. Living a stress free life takes work. In MS and almost any other illness that comes to mind I expect that being stress free will be a piece to the puzzle. Research has proven time and again that stress is detrimental to our minds, our bodies and our well-being.

Following the two episodes described above, head to toe numbness and optic neuritis I had a third attack. Here again I was under extreme stress. Let me paint a picture for you, I was working full time in an office performing a position normally held by a man. Maybe a lot of my stress was self-imposed and maybe I felt I was being overly scrutinized, maybe it was a little of both. I put in a minimum of 45 hours a week, occasional Saturdays and almost daily overtime. I know I was of great employee with a great attendance record and a great work record. When I was eventually laid off I still held the best attendance record in the company. Driven. I also worked weekends at a banquet hall bartending for weddings and special occasions. Often times there was a weekday wedding, so I would work that also. In addition to working two jobs I attended night school two nights a week. You see, I was trying to put money into my 401(k), save for a house (I am single) and further my job training hopefully qualifying for a higher salaried position. In between jobs I would grab something to eat and a shower if I had time. If there was no time I would take my shower in the morning before work and just get up earlier. Note: I'm still dealing with excess tiredness coupled with the stress of two jobs and night school, and then getting up an hour earlier just to take a shower or maybe do a load of laundry.

I began having bad backaches and numbness in both thighs so I tried chiropractic treatments for several years until the chiropractor suggested that I see a neurologist. After a MRI scan I was told I was dealing with MS.

Six years after diagnosis I now need a cane to steady myself while walking. In hindsight, and if you don't already walk with a cane please think about it. I let my pride stop me from buying and using a cane far longer than when I started to need one. I felt I was too young to be walking with a cane and I also felt embarrassed. I know now that if I had started walking with a cane sooner and walking more and further I would have preserved more muscle memory and muscle strength. My back would have remained stronger longer. At that time neurologists were telling patients to take it easy, don't exert yourself, don't overheat yourself, be very careful when you exercise, get lots of rest, and on and on. Heeding that advice contributed to a steady decline for me. You know what they say "hindsight is 20/20". Babying myself so much also caused my weight to balloon to 220 lbs. I went a high protein diet which gave me a big weight loss but strangely made the MS symptoms worsen. Diet was a piece to my puzzle, but I didn't know it.

For about a year after diagnosis I continued to work two jobs and go to night school. One evening at my part-time job I lost my balance and fell. I broke my wrist and that ended my part-time job and night school both. In my heart, I was still very proud of myself for trying. There is a common thread with most people that I meet dealing with MS, they are overachievers. They are driven. I hope and pray that there is an epiphany forming in your spirit, for it is this drive that will cause you to triumph over this adversity. When you 'get it', that there IS a way out you'll become driven again.

I spent 13 years working at a company that I thought I might only last three or four years at. When I stopped working 5 years ago I was actually relieved that I was being laid off because I would have just continued to force myself to go to work every day eight or nine hours a day until I was stopped. I had fallen at work a few times and I know that my supervisor was concerned that I would hurt myself.

After being laid off I continued to live by myself and do the best I could. Once again in hindsight, I now see and understand that exercise is a piece of my puzzle. It is a piece of everyone's puzzle. I was never a person who enjoyed exercising, I enjoyed working. I enjoyed making my own money. I grew up not having very much and so when I became old enough to work, I worked. Working allowed me to buy things. Coming from a family of six I had a lot of hand-me-downs. Working allowed me to have brand new things.

Working allowed me to have some of the things I dreamed of. And so I loved to work. If I had things to do over, I would have balanced work, exercise and fun.

A little over a year ago I met Ramon in the MS support group that he administrated on Facebook. Since then, he has been mentoring me in exercise, muscle memory, PMA and in the things I could do for myself to improve.

There are so many things that I didn't understand about what was happening in my brain and my body. I know doctors and researchers have a far greater understanding of how MS works yet none of this is taught to the people (patients) that are dealing with it. Ramon probably has a greater understanding because he spent so much time in OT and PT. He also spent time bedridden, paralyzed from the neck down. He needed to work harder and he had so much further to go then I had. He had trained professionals working with him every day and he asked lots and lots of questions. He worked out some of his theories on PT. He was very driven to not only understand what was happening but then to conquer it. When I met him and heard his story I knew I had met someone with the wisdom and knowledge to help me win my battle. As the adopted son of a pastor and his wife, he was the perfect mix of Godliness and wisdom for me in order to fuel a great PMA.

I'm proud to say that this past year has produced great accomplishments. Progress never comes as fast as you would like it to but for me, progress has been in baby steps. This past year I started driving again although I'm not comfortable going alone, that will come in time. A few months back my neurologist took me off of Tecfidera. Prior to this I had been on Copaxone for about seven years. I was downgraded from SPMS to RRMS and told that MS is no longer active for me. I don't know about you, but I've never heard of this. Don't misunderstand, I still have a lot of work to do. I still exercise daily. I no longer fear stairs. I am careful with my diet daily. For me, fatigue is no longer a daily issue but rather occasional. I still use a walker in the house. When I leave the house I use a wheelchair which I believe will not be forever. Ramon helped me to see that doing things like wall walking and using a cane when I really needed a walker was not helping me. It was hurting me. It was making everything more difficult and causing more strain for me to just get around. It did nothing for my strength, especially the back muscles and nothing for my leg muscles. My balance was continuing to decline as I was completely unaware that balance was capable of improving with the right exercise, the right movements and a PMA (positive mental attitude).

This past year has also produced a new understanding for me. After 20+ years of listening to doctors, researchers and other patients discuss the decline that accompanies MS, I was unaware that there was another way of looking at it. Occasionally I had heard a story or two of someone who had regained their health after battling MS, but it was rare. In the past year I've heard of this happening at least once a week. For me it's not a battle that can't be won and it's not a death sentence. It took a change of attitude, a diet change (I had already started on this a few years back) and the addition of targeted exercises that would produce the results that I needed to strengthen my body. In the first edition of **No More MS Depression** I mentioned that if (and I believe this will happen) there is a cure found, the cure would not enable patients to just stand up and start walking overnight. Those that have been exercising all along will have the strength and stability in their bodies to do this. Those that haven't will be battling atrophy and a road back that will take much more time.

With or without a cure on the horizon there is no time to waste. Your body is capable of healing itself and people like Ramon have come back from a worse place then I am in to beat this and I will too. I have proved in my own body and in my own mind that this can be reversed.

I am still taking Ampyra and LDN (Low Dose Naltrexone). And I watch the news stories on the Internet and television to stay current on the research regarding a cure and also on the drugs they are working on. It seems to me the best hope for a complete reversal of disability is going to lie in stem cell research. From all the indications that will be soon. Once the myelin sheath is repaired and the connections are restored, it will STILL take diet, exercise and a great PMA. If/when you make MS incapable of getting a foothold but DON'T change your diet, exercise and PMA what do think might be NEXT in line to attack you? Heart disease? A tumor? Cancer? Lupus?

I have in mind my personal thoughts on how MS operates. In my mind it is a cascading syndrome. There is no other way to explain how thousands of patients with the same diagnosis can vary so greatly. The syndrome seems to start slowly and when I say slowly I believe a lot don't even notice or won't admit that it started. But it starts. Part of the diagnosis of MS includes medical history. What the neurologist is listening for is a pattern. He or she is listening for neurologically based complaints that have been periodically happening over time. For me personally, it was three incidences over a 15 year period that were unable to be explained or labeled. The three incidences, and there can be more or less, were all neurologically based. Most neurologists will couple this suspicion along with one or several of the following: blood test, MRI, spinal tap, physical exam. An MRI all by itself does not necessarily indicate MS. Patients have mentioned that they feel this is how the diagnosis was made, but the fact is brain lesions are present in other conditions as well as in completely healthy individuals. They still do not completely understand how some brain lesions exist and produce zero symptoms. Use this piece of information as a tool to put in your toolbox. Whenever you have an MRI done, don't let the MRI report upset you. Ramon will tell you that after his first MRI they found 37 lesions and at his most recent MRI that number had been slashed by two thirds. Again, the body can heal itself. The brain heals itself. Diet, exercise and PMA.

Your toolbox will look like no one else's and only you know how many tools are in it. You are going to create a virtual toolbox in your mind (or in your computer) and you are going to start looking for the tools to put the pieces of your puzzle back together. You are going to look everywhere. You are going to pay attention. You are going to listen for wisdom that applies to you. The MS that you deal with is specific to you. When you finish figuring out your puzzle you will have designed a whole new healthy life and way of living for yourself. MS may or may not try to attack you again but it will not be able to. I know for myself, that I have caused a big enough turn around in my own life as well as the knowledge I have gained in understanding MS that it could never again gain the foothold in my life that it once had. I'll bet money that Ramon feels the same.

READING NOTES

CHAPTER 19

MOVE ON PURPOSE WITH A PURPOSE

By Jackie E. Joy

If you are unfamiliar with Tai Chi then I implore you to do a little research and educate yourself on this ancient Chinese form of martial arts. Let me clarify, I'm not asking that you consider taking up tai chi, I'm asking that you research it and attempt to assimilate the philosophy here-in as a tool to help your own body. Although tai chi is considered a "soft" martial art, the health benefits and especially the improvement in balance are immeasurable. There are three aspects to tai chi: health, meditation and self-defense. In China tai chi is practiced in large open areas, especially parks by people of all ages. Tai chi is world renowned for improving balance and health particularly in the elderly. In growing older one of the first senses to decline is balance. Once an individual starts to lose their sense of balance, their overall health goes into a declining cascade. Sounds a little like MS? Loss of balance produces fear which produces an overly cautious nature which contributes to falls which contributes to injuries which contributes to more fear which contributes to less activity which contributes to more disability and on and on. And you may or may not know that the Chinese emperor strongly recommends that its citizens practice daily to safeguard their health and to heal a variety of infirmities.

I'm asking you to Google tai chi and watch and listen. I want you to listen to the philosophy and the purpose with which tai chi is taught and practiced. I want you to watch the movement, the speed of movement. As you watch and listen you will begin to formulate tools from what you are seeing and hearing. If you will incorporate these tools in dealing with MS and starting to move on purpose with a purpose, not only will your health improve but your muscles and body strength will improve. There is a couple thousand years of proof for the benefits that tai chi produces.

This knowledge is part of your exercise tools in your toolbox. Exercising your muscles will improve your balance and improving your balance will exercise your muscles. It all works together. Tai chi also incorporates meditation for it is necessary to concentrate (meditate) on your legs, torso, arms, neck and head all at once in slow motion as well as muscles (and for us, balance also). You will begin to discover that slowing down takes all your concentration and all your strength thereby working out your muscles. For years I hurried. With limited energy and limited strength in my body I hurried to get as much done as possible before I ran out of energy. And now I see that the opposite of what I was doing would be twice as productive. By slowing down I improved my balance and therefore my strength and therefore my productivity.

Tai chi is a series of controlled movements. Slow movements. Movements incorporating balance. More advanced forms of tai chi incorporate advanced strength and advanced forms of balance. Meditating and focusing on your body while moving will take practice and practice will produce a habit. Hopefully by now you have already set in your mind that the MS that you deal with is temporary. Therefore building a habit of meditating on movement and balance to build strength as you age is a great plan. Don't you think so?

Yoga is another mind/body/spirit discipline. I've heard lots of people dealing with MS do Yoga. There is even chair-yoga.

When Ramon had me put down my cane and stop wall walking I did it by faith. Here was a person that was totally bedridden after a MS attack now coaching me. I had a walker with two wheels on it. I purchased a four wheel walker. What I found out was that it took a lot of strength in my torso to push the walker, stop it, hold it still, walk forward and then push it again. After months of using my walker it became easier and I became stronger. My back became muscular. Beware and be aware of things becoming too easy. Again, this goes against what my doctor has been telling me. When things become easy that is the time to push yourself harder and reach further. You are getting closer to your goals.

After I was diagnosed I searched out MS support groups. I attended a couple meetings. I felt in my heart that this wasn't for me because I was not willing to "learn to live with" this. In my home I have adaptive equipment to keep myself safe. I have had my washer and dryer brought up from the basement because it became unsafe for me. I have had my bathroom remodeled complete with a step in shower, grab bars and an ADA height toilet all to keep myself safe. In the past years I have fallen enough and hurt myself enough to know that injuries set me back months. I do not wish to waste any more time recovering from injuries that could have been prevented in the first place. I have lofty goals and no time to waste. I have all of these conveniences to 'keep me safe' NOT to help me 'learn to live with this'. PMA!

There is another "functional movement" method called Feldenkrais. I would like you to Google this also. Feldenkrais is a type of therapy (for lack of a better description) that involves concentration while moving. Like tai chi, Feldenkrais will improve balance and strength.

With both of these philosophies there are numerous Google sites as well as YouTube videos available. Please take the time to search these out and incorporate some of the ideas into your day. You will derive benefits. Any of these philosophies can be incorporated whether you are bedridden with extremely limited movement capability, in a wheelchair or walking with limitations. There are tools here for everyone.

READING NOTES

CHAPTER 20

BREAKFAST

By Jackie E. Joy

The main purpose for this chapter is mainly to get you thinking about breakfast. Breakfast is referred to as "the most important meal of the day" for this reason and also because we deal with MS, breakfast should be the very first meal that you scrutinize and get right.

The word breakfast is made up of two words "break" and "fast" which means to "break the fast"- of the night. There are anywhere between seven and 12 hours from the time you ate dinner the previous day to your breakfast the following morning. This is a fast. Whenever you think about breakfast or what you are going to have for breakfast or where you are going to go for breakfast, you are going to now think of "breaking the fast". Fasting in itself is beneficial. Lots of books are written on fasting and there are thousands of websites on fasting. During the night while "fasting" your mind and body is resting, rejuvenating, cleansing and preparing itself for another day of activity. It is also healing.

While researching fasting you will find that the very best way to "break the fast" is with a glass of water. Very simple. Very cleansing. After 7 to 12 hours of eating and drinking nothing your tissues need clean water. You may live in a city that has very good tap water or you may prefer bottled water or even filtered water, do your own research. In the city where I live a water quality test report is included with my water bill so I am aware of my water quality. Even so, I am interested in a good quality filtration system reasonably priced, so I am always searching information on water systems for myself.

I use a large cup (about 20 ounces) for my morning water. I prefer my water cool or even cold but not room temperature. If you have studied macrobiotics at all, macrobiotics teaches that your water should be closer to room temperature. But I prefer it cool. In reading this book and thinking about the water you drink I hope that by now you became aware of a theme, namely research everything and find what works best for you. That is going to be the bottom line as to how you find the pieces to your puzzle. Listen to everybody, read everything, research everything, try a lot of things and discover what works best for you. Now let me expand a little bit on my breakfast and this is not because I am claiming that I have found what works best but it is because I want you to figure out the best breakfast for you. In my large glass of water I add one heaping tablespoon of MSM (methylsulfonylmethane) which is important for detoxification and helps in conditions where there is inflammation. MSM is 34% sulfur which is one of the elements of greatest benefits in foods like broccoli, kale, mustard greens and cabbage. Once again, do a little research on MSM. To my glass of water I also add between a quarter to a half teaspoon of D-Mannose powder. NOTE: D-Mannose comes in powder form at a fraction of the cost of tablets. Save your money. If you have a great neurologist who is up on nutritional information and you have been struggling with bladder infections, he/she may have mentioned D-Mannose. I add one more item and that is diatomaceous earth. I can't repeat this enough that you research what works best for you and with everything that you're doing to help you know why. Diatomaceous earth MUST be food grade and, I feel is a very cheap substance in return for all the benefits it delivers.

In the first book MS-101 in chapter 7 on Diet I mentioned sprouting. Sprouts are part of my breakfast along with a tablespoon of organic honey and personally I find growing and taking care of sprouts a small investment of time considering the large contribution of vitamins and minerals that it contributes. If I were juicing my breakfast then this would be a great addition also. Sprouts are easy to digest and pack big nutritional benefits in a little package. In studying Dr. Terry Wahl's books on Paleo diets I see that sulfur rich foods are of highest nutritional benefits for us so I choose to include broccoli, kale, mustard greens, cabbage and a few others for sprouting.

In addition to a large cup of water followed by sprouts and honey I usually have fruit and I follow all of that with seeds. I like having sunflower seeds and pumpkin seeds, just a tablespoon of each.

I implore you to look at your breakfast as it is the most important meal of the day, it starts your day and depending on how nutritionally rich it is, I feel will affect your day. It certainly will affect your energy level.

READING NOTES

CHAPTER 21

DIETS AND HOW I COOK

My method of cooking comes from a mother and father who always dared to make what I and many around me call "MUSH". But I take what I have learned and what my culinary school taught me and I look for the best healthy options. I do have to tell you that Dr. Terry L Wahls and her books on what she has done with the Paleo diet is a huge inspiration to me.

Just so you know, my cooking style is Soul "from my parents" Latin "because I'm Puerto Rican" and French "because I attended LA Cordon Bleu" C.H.I.C. in Chicago and although I did not graduate unfortunately, I went as a hobby anyway not a career and I just LOVE to cook. So I attended to learn new ways to cook and I did.

Now I feel I can cook ANYTHING. I try NEW stuff all the time, as well as taking old recipes that I learned from my mother who is 87 now and grew up on a farm in Baton Rouge, LA. My father was from Biloxi, MS so southern and African American <black, as my parents and I were not fond of that term African American since they were born here> Hispanic, I learned a lot from YouTube and the times I watched Miss Mendez cook who I call my 3rd mother.

So I took what I had learned from my 3 sources and started to figure out how I could make healthy alternatives to the FATTY comfort foods that I grew up on. I am still trying new things for myself and my roommate Jackie Joy, but there are no complaints at ALL and we still have not gained any weight and our lab number's <blood tests> are better than ever, so in short I did it for me and I see it working well for someone OTHER than me. So for me, finding this piece to my puzzle worked out GREAT, not only can we now eat almost whatever we want, we can do it without feeling guilty and without feeding negative nutrition into our cells which in turn feeds Multiple Sclerosis.

Now I'm going to replace a few items in recipes with what I use as healthy alternatives containing low to zero GMO's and or gluten:

#1 TOSTONES <fried plantains>

3 TBSP canola oil for frying <pan frying>

2 green plantains, peeled and sliced (1/4 in.)
1/2 teaspoon sea salt

I use canola oil because it's the HEALTHIER alternative to other oils with a high enough smoking point.

<<MEANING you can cook this oil at a higher heat without breaking the oil down>>

#2 CHEESY SPAGHETTI

1 (16 ounce) package spaghetti <gluten free or rice noodles>
2 pounds ground beef <Farm raised>
1/4 cup chopped onion <Organic or from your own garden>
2 (26.5 ounce) cans meatless spaghetti sauce <gluten free, hard to find GMO free OR make your own>
1 (16 ounce) container fat-free sour cream <still looking>

2 cups shredded mozzarella cheese, divided <still looking for alternative>

1/2 cup Parmesan cheese <still looking for alternative>

Salt and black pepper to taste <use fresh ground pepper and sea salt has trace minerals and nutrients and body absorbs and gets rid of it faster>

#3 FRIED CHICKEN

2 packets of chicken thighs and or breasts <Farm Raised>

Deep fryer with 2 to 3 quarts of Canola Oil <See above>

Bar-B-Que sauce <your choice I use Sweet Baby Rays>

Fry for 25 mins. Then brush on Bar-B-Que to taste

#4 BROCCOLI

3 tablespoons sesame seeds <many health benefits to this>

2 tablespoons rice vinegar <or any vinegar, not only does it have a lot of health benefits but it helps to expel body fat>

1 tablespoon dark sesame oil

1 tablespoon lower-sodium soy sauce <or an organic or Liquid Aminos (Bragg)>

1 (12-ounce) package fresh broccoli florets <organic>

These are a few I have found and made healthy for me. It's just a few examples and there is a WORLD of new ways to do them, PLEASE do what best for YOUR diet and battle with MS. This book is my ideas and are not meant as a golden standard but only as a guide to show people how I have won and what pieces I used in my battle against MS. So one day I pray to see YOUR guidelines so I can build on them and we ALL can finally say MS IS OVER.

READING NOTES

CHAPTER 22

MORE QUOTES

#1 IF you run after what's in front of you, you distance yourself from what's behind YOU! ~~ Bishop Jakes (Pastor 2014)

#2 Success is NEVER an accident, you must work for it! ~~ Bishop Jakes (Pastor 2014)

#3 Misery always precedes the moment. After you have suffered a while... Survive your misery so you can have your moment.~~ Bishop Jakes (Pastor 2014)

#4 In the middle of difficulty lies opportunity.~~Albert Einstein, PhD (Genius, Physicist, 1879-1955)

#5 Whether you think you can, or think you can't, you're probably right.~~Henry Ford (Founder, Ford Motor Co. 1863-1947)

#6 Many of life's failures are people who did not realize how close they were to success when they gave up.~~Thomas Edison (Inventor, 1847-1931)

#7 When people hurt you over and over, think of them like sandpaper. They may scratch and hurt you a bit, but in the end, you end up polished and they end up useless.~~Chris Colfer (Actor, singer, 1990-)

#8 Surround yourself with only people who are going to lift you higher.~~Oprah Winfrey (Business woman, 1954)

#9 A false friend and a shadow attend only while the sun shines.~~Benjamin Franklin (6th US president, 1706-1790)

#10 Your perception goes a long way in determining what your life is like. Is the glass half empty or is the glass half full.~~Russ Stiffler

#11 When you come to the end of your rope, tie a knot and hang on.~~Franklin D. Roosevelt

#12 Sometimes you have to wreck what was FORMER to make the NEW!~~Pastor T.D Jakes

#13 IF you do not have a sense of sacrifice you lose you sense of success.~~Pastor T.D Jakes

#14 ALWAYS ask a question. Those who care will HELP you find the answers! Those who don't have an answer.~~Ramon Hyron Garcia

#15 BE of a sound mind and your day will play a BEAUTIFUL HARMONY.~~Ramon Hyron Garcia

#16 YOU are 5% of what you think! 5% of what you say! 90% on how you act"!~~Ramon Hyron Garcia

#17 The ULTIMATE deception is allowing ones self-focus to be redirected to an issue OTHER than the one you were focused on!~~Ramon Hyron Garcia

#18 THINGS seem bleak to those that LOOK at the hallway instead of the door in front of them!~~Ramon Hyron Garcia

#19 One of the MANY problems with LYING... THAT person will start to think it's TRUTH!~~Ramon Hyron Garcia

#20 A dream is the story you're ABOUT to write out in LIFE! Never stop!~~Ramon Hyron Garcia

READING NOTES

CHAPTER 23

DEDICATION

Jackie Joy has been my rock and my encouragement for over a year now. She has taught me that even in the face of ugliness I need to find the beauty. She to me is a hero. A person who looked upon the fires that consumed her and took it with a smile on her face and knew she did not know how the future would be BUT this would not stop her from reaching out and lending a helping hand to a fellow man who was sinking. She has shown me to NEVER give up even when you are winning and to push harder because it's not over until it is OVER.

To understand, that even at my best I will tell you it is not good enough and perfect what you thought was perfect. I write now and dedicate this book to a woman who not only pushed me into writing but also was brave enough to correct me when I thought I was making the right choice. Yes, Jackie Joy is my friend, NO wait, she's like my OLDER sister whom I could NEVER repay for her kindness and the blessings she poured on and into me. IF and when I have a daughter, I pray that she ends up as 1/2 the woman I know to be Jackie Joy.

There are NO truer words to explain the woman she is so all I can do is keep her in my thoughts, my heart and my writings. You will NEVER be alone and NEVER be forgotten! Keep that smile and know that I helped you get cable, a new couch, computer, etc., WELCOME TO THE 21st century! =p